SOUTH WEST
INDEPENDENT
COFFEE
GUIDE

the INSIDER'S GUIDE TO THE BEST INDY
COFFEE VENUES AND ROASTERS

★ ★ ★ ★ ★ ★ ★ ★ ★ ★ ★

Salt Media, 5 Cross Street, Devon, EX31 1BA.
www.saltmedia.co.uk
Tel: 01271 859299
Email: info@saltmedia.co.uk

Salt Media coffee guide team: Jo Rees,
Nick Cooper, Catherine Jones, Chris Sheppard,
Dan Riordan, Tamsin Powell, Gemma Chilton,
Sarah Orme and Kathryn Lewis
Design: Salt Media
Illustrations: Jose Walker

Photo: Tom Powell

> TODAY'S BREW
> COUNTRY: COLO
> FARM: PESCA
> VARIETY: ——
> PROCESS: WA
> EXPECT: CLEAN
> SWEET.

FOREWORD

We're in the middle of a coffee revolution. Cold brew, single origin beans from named estates, focus on flavour profiles and a meeting of science and art are all part of coffee's Fourth Wave. And the South West is perfectly placed to ride it – we're used to waves after all.

This, the first ever *South West Independent Coffee Guide*, has emerged from a vibrant South West speciality coffee scene that celebrates the local and the artisan. The venues and roasters are small, bespoke and owner-operated, and the community wants to share the experience! I hope you enjoy exploring this wonderland of flavours – at around £2.50 a cup, you can afford to be brave and dive right in.

'THE MOVEMENT CELEBRATES WHAT'S LOCAL AND ARTISAN, AS THE VENUES AND ROASTERS ARE SMALL-SCALE AND BESPOKE'

A huge thank you goes to our lead sponsor, Yeo Valley, for supporting the guide, along with Clifton Coffee Roasters, Origin Coffee Roasters, Bunn, Coffee Hit, Mahlkonig and La Spaziale. It's been an exhilarating journey.

Jo Rees
Editor, food Insider's Guides

www.food-mag.co.uk
🐦/@rees_jo
🐦/@Indycoffeeguide
🐦/@food_mag

Yeo Valley FAMILY FARM

organic

Whole Milk

Naturally delicious

For dreamy creamy coff

Love your coffee, love our milk

Supporting British Family Farms

TO FIND OUT MORE ABOUT OUR FAMILY FARM
VISIT YEOVALLEY.CO.UK

CONTENTS

12   WELCOME

14   WHOLE LATTE LOVE

16   A WORLD OF COFFEE

19   THE VENUES

20   SOUTH WEST MAP

22   GLOUCESTERSHIRE & BATH

32   SOMERSET & BRISTOL

50   DORSET

56   DEVON

74   CORNWALL

84   MORE GOOD CUPS

86   THE ART OF THE BARISTA

88   BREWING UP HISTORY

91   THE ROASTERS

92   A TOAST TO THE ROASTERS

113   MEET THE COMMITTEE

MAXWELL
COLONNA-DASHWOOD

WELCOME
TO OUR WORLD OF COFFEE

Putting something like the *South West Independent Coffee Guide* together involves a lot of planning and thought, and what soon became apparent in the many conversations we had, was how there's been a paradigm shift in our relationship with coffee.

The South West has quietly and determinedly become a nuanced and exciting coffee landscape, driven by the development of a cohesive speciality coffee market. At its heart, speciality coffee is like the world of wine in that it focuses on provenance and character. Carefully considered beverages have provided the backbone of the movement and so there's focus on every part of the journey of the coffee bean, from its harvesting as the seed of a cherry, grown and tended to at lofty elevations around the globe, to the roasting and brewing of the bean itself.

The resulting drink reflects this attention to detail and interest in what makes coffee taste so varied and unique, which is why you'll find many coffee offerings accompanied by individual flavour and tasting notes.

'THE VENUES IN THIS GUIDE – AND THE GUIDE ITSELF – REPRESENT THE EMERGENCE OF "COFFEE TOURISM"'

The way coffee is now being presented is changing at quite a pace, but its history as a powerful cultural and social stimulant will always be significant. The coffee shops in this guide represent spaces in which to pass through or to sit and ponder, places to meet and chat. It's easy to see why coffee shops are often termed our "third place" (after home and work) and daily interaction with coffee shops is becoming increasingly entwined with our lives.

As well as providing a break in our daily routines, the venues in this guide – and the guide itself – represent the emergence of "coffee tourism". After all, guidebooks have led people to new and exciting realms for centuries. So, whether it's a quick detour to pop into a well known coffee shop, or a planned visit to make the most of what's on offer in the South West, I urge you to grab your guide and start planning an adventure!

Maxwell Colonna-Dashwood
UK Barista Champion and director of Colonna & Small's, Bath
/@colonna_smalls

WHOLE LATTE LOVE

THE FOURTH WAVE OF THE COFFEE REVOLUTION CELEBRATES INGREDIENTS FROM SPECIFIC REGIONS THAT HAVE BEEN CAREFULLY SOURCED. WE THINK THE QUALITY OF MILK IS JUST SUCH AN INGREDIENT, WHICH IS WHY IT WAS BRILLIANT TO SEE YEO VALLEY'S ORGANIC MILK FROM THE SOUTH WEST COME TOP IN A NATIONAL SURVEY OF THE BEST MILK FOR COFFEE ...

Last year *The Grocer* magazine consulted baristas and coffee shops Harris + Hoole, and ran a series of blind taste tests on different brands of milk. The aim was to find the best milk for making espresso-based coffee drinks. Andrew Tolley, coffee director of Harris + Hoole, said *'Yeo Valley's milk simply stood out as tasting better with a blend of Columbia 70 per cent and Costa Rica 30 per cent,'* while Ben Townsend of the London School of Coffee commented that it *'worked well to balance the coffee.'* Back in the South West, Simon Buckingham, head of drink at Boston Tea Party, said *'We tested a number of milks that met our criteria, and Yeo Valley's milk was the best for consistency and flavour. It's easier for milk texturing and, most importantly, it tastes great.'*

Priding itself on its ethical approach, Yeo Valley is definitely a dairy for the South West to be proud of. The main family farm lies at the foot of the Mendip Hills and has been owned and run by the Meads since 1961. There's another farm, just four miles away, up on the Mendips and together the two sites cover 1,200 acres of land and share an award-winning herd of 420 british friesian cows.

Yeo Valley describes its milk as '100 per cent Yeoganic', which means it goes the extra mile to look after its livestock and to be ethical and sustainable. As owner Tim Mead says, *'Supporting British family farms is at the heart of everything we do, which includes buying British produce where we can, and supporting other small dairy farmers. So all our milk is supplied through the South West-based Organic Milk Suppliers Co-operative (OMSCo). By working together we are able to help lots of smaller family farms keep going.'* It also explains why Yeo Valley splits its own herd into two separate farms. As Tim explains, *'Smaller herds mean happier, healthier cows.'*

The team cares deeply about the entire milking process, from looking after its cows, to the food they're fed and the impact on the environment. There's even a conservation team that spends its days dry stone walling, tree planting and hedge laying. *'We operate a rotational farming model, which means that not only do we grow grass for our cows to eat, we grow our own cereals too. Doing all of this means that only great food goes into our cows, and then of course, only great milk comes out.'*

'IT'S EASIER FOR MILK TEXTURING AND, MOST IMPORTANTLY, IT TASTES GREAT'

A WORLD OF COFFEE
TOP 10
PRODUCERS
(AND FACT SHOTS)

10/MEXICO
3,800*

4,600*
7/HONDURAS

3/COLUMBIA
11,000*

Commercial coffee cultivation requires very specific environmental conditions – with the majority of the world's supplies produced in a geographic belt along the sub-tropics and high-altitude moist tropics.

In general, coffee growing requires an annual rainfall of 1500-3000mm, with ideal average temperatures ranging from 15-30ºC, depending on the bean variety. All coffee is easily damaged by frost.

8/PERU
4,250*

53,700*
1/BRAZIL

*****PRODUCTION OF THOUSAND 60KG BAGS**
SOURCE: UNITED STATES DEPARTMENT OF AGRICULTURE (2013/14)

BRAZILIAN COFFEE BEANS ARE MILD WITH LOW ACIDITY, MAKING THEM THE MOST ACCESSIBLE AND POPULAR IN THE WORLD

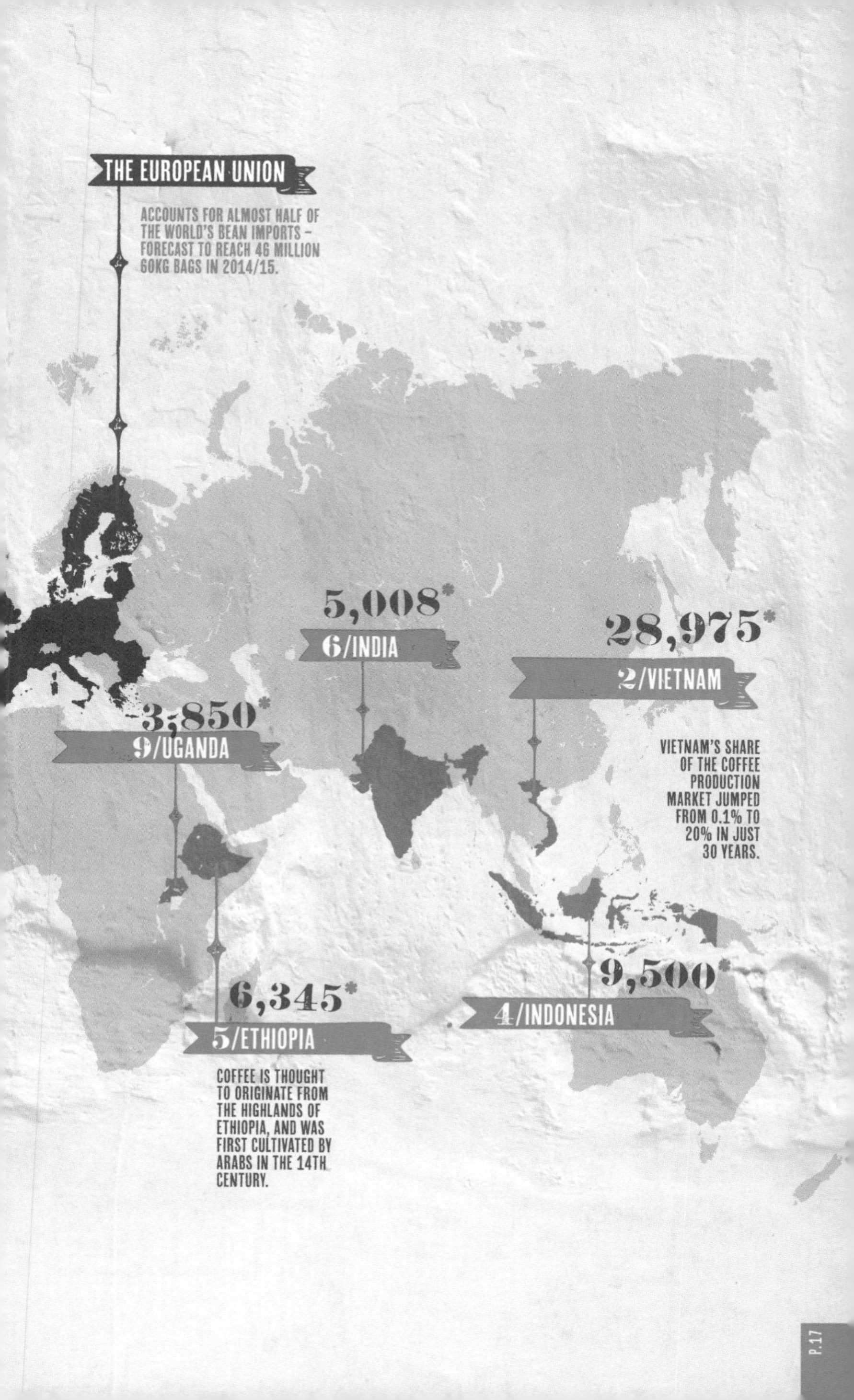

THE EUROPEAN UNION

ACCOUNTS FOR ALMOST HALF OF
THE WORLD'S BEAN IMPORTS –
FORECAST TO REACH 46 MILLION
60KG BAGS IN 2014/15.

5,008*
6/INDIA

28,975*
2/VIETNAM

VIETNAM'S SHARE
OF THE COFFEE
PRODUCTION
MARKET JUMPED
FROM 0.1% TO
20% IN JUST
30 YEARS.

3,850*
9/UGANDA

6,345*
5/ETHIOPIA

9,500*
4/INDONESIA

COFFEE IS THOUGHT
TO ORIGINATE FROM
THE HIGHLANDS OF
ETHIOPIA, AND WAS
FIRST CULTIVATED BY
ARABS IN THE 14TH
CENTURY.

THE VENUES

YOU ARE HERE

2 COFFEE VENUE

49 MOBILE COFFEE VENUE

88 ROASTER

3 MORE GOOD CUPS

DEVON

31 **30**

32

EXETER
SEE PAGE 57 FOR CITY MAP

42

69

CORNWALL

44
45
43

39

40

76

46

41

72
49

81
47 **48**
70 **71** **83**

50

Locations are approximate

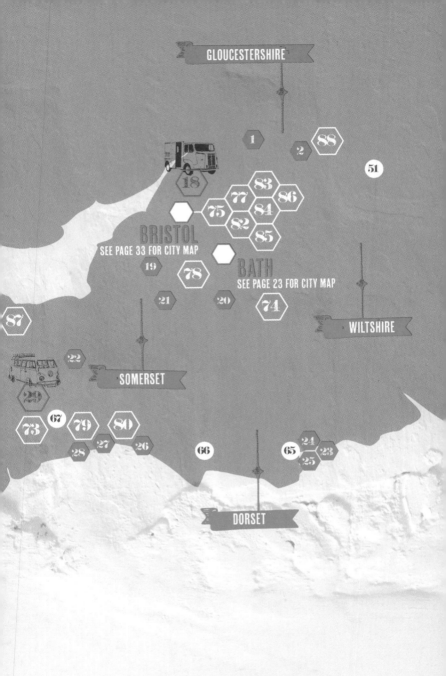

GLOUCESTERSHIRE

1

2

88

51

18

83

77

75

86

84

82

85

BRISTOL
SEE PAGE 33 FOR CITY MAP

19

78

BATH
SEE PAGE 23 FOR CITY MAP

21

20

74

WILTSHIRE

87

22

SOMERSET

29

73

67

79

80

28

27

26

66

65

24

23

25

DORSET

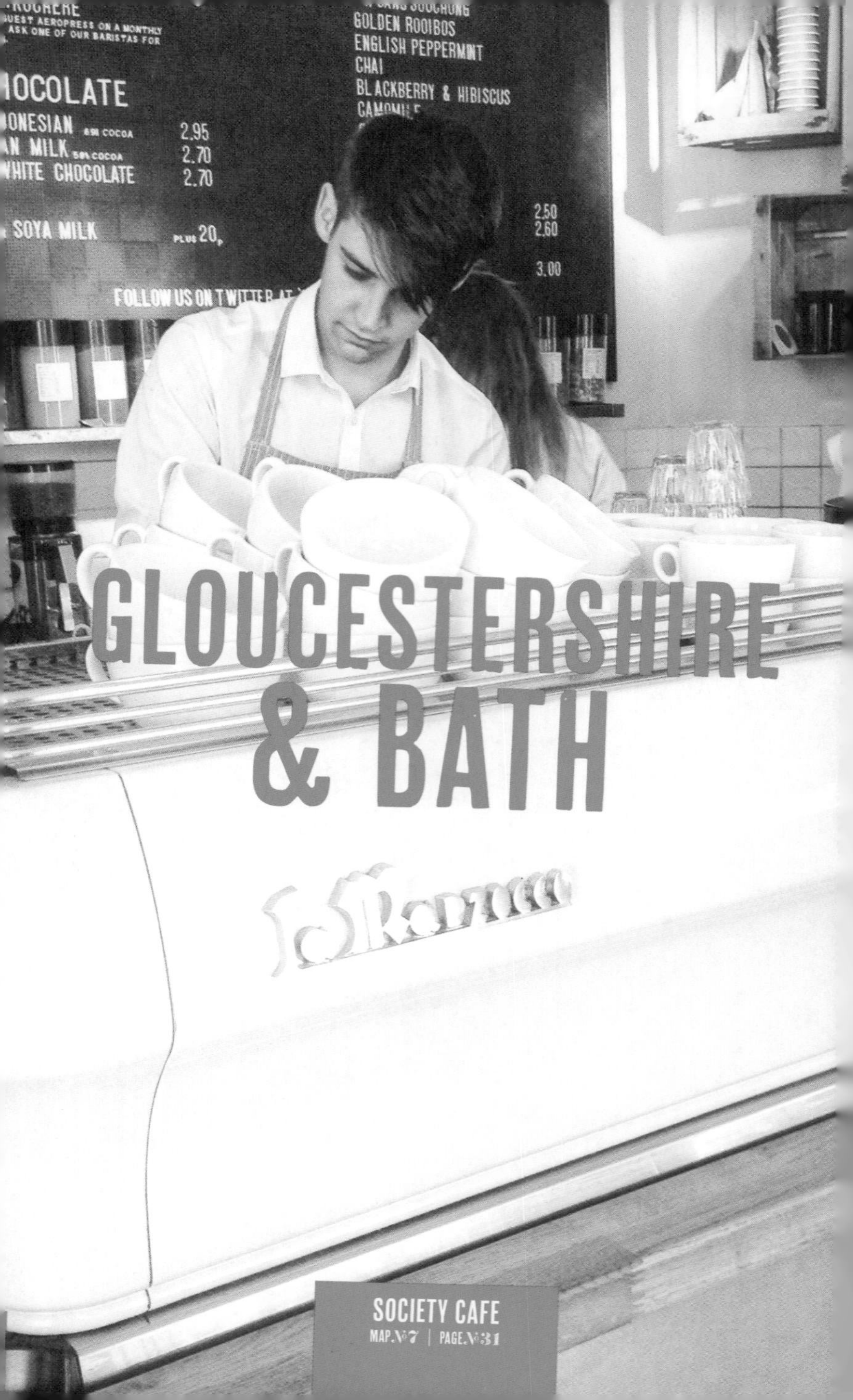

GLOUCESTERSHIRE & BATH

SOCIETY CAFE
MAP.№7 | PAGE.№31

BATH

QUEEN SQUARE

54

Milsom Street

Broad Street

3

River Avon

PULTENEY BRIDGE

A4

5

4

6

Westgate Street

BATH ABBEY

7

James Street West

ROMAN BATHS

North Parade

53

A3039

Lower Bristol Road

52

COFFEE VENUE

MORE GOOD CUPS

1. STAR ANISE ARTS CAFE

1 Gloucester Street, Stroud, Gloucestershire, GL5 1QG.

Hidden away from the hustle and bustle of Stroud's high street, is the refreshingly creative Star Anise Arts Cafe. Its team got into speciality coffee after deciding that what was on offer at the cafe didn't match the standard of the locally sourced, organic food it is celebrated for. So they paired up with Extract Coffee Roasters and got fully trained up. The result? A cafe that's now as loved for its coffee as for its food – plus a loyal band of regulars who

INSIDERS TIP IT SERVES THE BEST CHOCOLATE AND AVOCADO CAKE, ANYWHERE!

visit daily for a dose of the black stuff. There are other attractions too at this artsy venue – local artwork lines the walls, live music and speakers feature regularly and you can watch the chefs cooking up a storm in the open kitchen. On sunny days, the lively atmosphere spills out into the courtyard, where lunch can be enjoyed alfresco with a drink from the licensed bar.

KEY ROASTER
Extract

BREWING METHODS
Espresso

MACHINE
Sanremo

GRINDER
Sanremo

OPENING HOURS
Mon-Fri 8am-5pm
Sat 8.30am-5pm

 Gluten FREE

 COFFEE BEANS AVAILABLE

 SOYA MILK AVAILABLE

 WIFI

 DISABLED ACCESS

 CYCLE FRIENDLY

 OUTDOOR SEATING

 FAMILY FRIENDLY

www.staraniseartscafe.com   T: 01453 840021

f/Star Anise Arts Cafe

2. COTSWOLD ARTISAN COFFEE

5 Bishop's Walk, Cricklade Street, Cirencester, Gloucestershire, GL7 1JH.

A true passion for coffee runs through every element of Cotswold Artisan Coffee – from owners Mandy and Barry Cook's energetic coffee chat to the interior of this Cirencester cafe. The Wega Concept All Black is the centrepiece, with simple black and white décor framing the machine and rustic canvas coffee bags draping the handmade bar. Mandy and Barry are keen to showcase great filter coffee and give their customers a choice of

INSIDERS TIP HEAD TO THE BREW BAR FOR A CHOICE OF THREE DIFFERENT BREW METHODS

steeping methods at the brew bar – and with six single origins to choose from, the combinations are intriguingly vast. The team works to a sustainable ethos, using organic, non-homogenised milk from the local dairy to complement the carefully selected coffee roasts, and home-grown ingredients wherever possible in its cakes and bakes. But it's the coffee courses and cupping sessions that make this place stand out. Take along your own equipment and let the highly trained staff show you how to produce quality coffee at home from your own gear.

KEY ROASTER
Multiple

BREWING METHODS
Espresso, V60, Clever dripper, AeroPress

MACHINE
Wega Concept All Black

GRINDER
Mazzer Super Jolly, Wega Compak, Macap MC5 deli grinder

OPENING HOURS
Mon-Sat 8am-5.30pm
Sun 10am-4pm
Subject to seasonal change – call if making a special journey

Gluten FREE

COFFEE BEANS AVAILABLE

SOYA MILK AVAILABLE

DISABLED ACCESS

COFFEE COURSES AVAILABLE

T: 01285 239327

/@cotsartcoffee

3. PICNIC COFFEE

9 Saracen Street, Bath, BA1 5BR.

Inspired by the Parisian cafe scene, owner Tim Starks runs Picnic Coffee with a truly continental perspective. Open until late three times a week, his Bath cafe has become quite a social hub in the evenings, where a quality coffee can be enjoyed alongside a glass of wine. Floor to ceiling windows mean it's bright and airy inside, with colourful furniture and quirky features to catch the eye, such as the coffee and chilli plants and a large selection of travel guides. Coffee tasting notes behind the bar guide you on your coffee explorations and there's a good selection of teas to be had, too. By day, Picnic is a place to catch up on some work or to break up a shopping trip by chilling on one of the inviting sofas with a cup of the house blend espresso and a handmade sandwich. It's family friendly and dogs are also welcome. By night, there's a lively mix of community events and jazz evenings, with local ales and ciders available.

INSIDERS TIP TIM'S ESPRESSO MARTINI IS A MUST-TRY

KEY ROASTER
Easy José

BREWING METHODS
Espresso,
AeroPress,
pourover and
cold brew

MACHINE
Sanremo
Verona TCS

GRINDER
Mahlkonig K30,
Mahlkonig Varios,
Quamar M80E

OPENING HOURS
Mon-Wed 7.30am-6pm
Thurs-Fri 7.30am-9pm
Sat 8.30am-9pm
Sun 9am-5pm

---

www.picniccoffee.co.uk   T: 07711 760013
f/Picnic Coffee   @picnic_bath

4. SOCIETY CAFE

19 High Street, Bath, BA1 5AJ.

Society Cafe, the little sister venture to one of Bath's most popular coffee spots, is a new addition to the city centre. Owners Adrian and Jane Campbell-Howard have boldly taken on the high street's big name coffee shops, and are keen to prove that you don't need to go off the beaten track to enjoy a quality cup. The quick stop shop possesses all of the original venue's character and charm, and its clean, sharp design echoes the serious caffeine ethos. Take-out is common practice here, whether for office workers, regulars or tourists in need of a caffeine boost, but there are also a few bar seats for those who want to linger. Grab one of the tasty sandwiches which are freshly prepared by Jane, or indulge your sweet tooth from the tempting range of cakes and pastries.

INSIDERS TIP THE TEAM'S PRIDE AND JOY IS A KOREAN RIDGE BREWER WHICH TAKES UP TO EIGHT HOURS TO PRODUCE A BATCH OF COLD BREW

KEY ROASTER
Round Hill

BREWING METHODS
AeroPress,
Clever dripper

MACHINE
La Marzocco
Linea PB

GRINDER
Mahlkonig K30 Twin
Vario and Mahlkonig
EK43

OPENING HOURS
Mon-Sat 7.30am-
6.30pm
Sun 10am-6pm

www.society-cafe.com   T: 01225 428008

f/Society Cafe   ✔/@societycafebath

MAP.N° 5. COLONNA & SMALL'S

6 Chapel Row, Bath, BA1 1HN.

The UK's top-rated barista is to be found behind an unassuming shop front on Bath's Queen Square. Inside, the cool, pared-back interior is where Maxwell Colonna-Dashwood – who won the 2014 UK Barista Championships – has created a wonderland of coffee that's become a must-visit destination for brew freaks and bean geeks. You'll find three espresso beans and three single origin/estate filter coffees on the brew bar on any given day. The coffee is exciting, challenges assumptions about the flavours one would expect to encounter, and of course tastes complex and delicious. The experience is enhanced by tasting notes on the board and flavour notes on what the espresso tastes like on its own, or with steamed milk. Warm and engaging chat from the knowledgeable baristas completes the experience and visitors can hang out in the cafe area, relax in the shady courtyard in warm weather or simply take a coffee to-go.

INSIDERS TIP MAXWELL ALSO RUNS COFFEE COURSES FOR HOME ENTHUSIASTS AND COFFEE PROS

KEY ROASTER
Round Hill,
Has Bean, Origin,
James Gourmet,
Tate, Workshop

BREWING METHODS
AeroPress,
Clever dripper,
syphon, cold brew,
Lungo brewed on the
espresso machine –
ground on the EK43

MACHINE
La Marzocco Strada

GRINDER
Nuova Simmonelli-
Mythos, Mahlkonig
k30 Twin,
Mahlkonig EK43

OPENING HOURS
Mon-Fri 8am-
5.30pm
Sat 8.30am-5.30pm
Sun 10am-4pm

Gluten FREE

COFFEE BEANS AVAILABLE

SOYA MILK AVAILABLE

WIFI

DISABLED ACCESS

COFFEE COURSES AVAILABLE

OUTDOOR seating

www.colonnaandsmalls.co.uk   T: 07766 808067

f/Colonna and Small's   /@colonna_smalls

6. BOSTON TEA PARTY

19 Kingsmead Square, Bath, BA1 2AE.

Boston Tea Party is a small, family-owned independent cafe group serving simple, well-prepared food and drinks made with quality ingredients.

The food and coffee are ethically sourced and everything is made from scratch onsite each day by people who clearly care about what they do.

Bath is the smallest (and possibly the busiest) cafe in the micro-chain, with rarely a spare seat and often a queue out of the door. Don't worry though, as there's plenty of outside seating on this busy square, which is great for a bit of people watching.

The coffee is as feel-good as the food and a range of artisan brews are available. Choose the dark house roast for flavours of cocoa, liquorice and toasted nuts or the medium house roast for a blast of chocolate, hazelnut and marmalade. Filter coffee is also available and the bean and roast changes monthly. Awarded a Sustainable Restaurant Association three (out of three) star rating.

KEY ROASTER
Extract

BREWING METHODS
Espresso and filter

MACHINE
La Marzocca

GRINDER
Mazzer Major

OPENING HOURS
Mon-Sat 7am-7.30pm
Sun 9am-7pm

INSIDERS TIP MONTHLY CHANGING SINGLE ESTATE FILTER COFFEE IS SUPPLIED BY BRISTOL-BASED ROASTERS EXTRACT

www.bostonteaparty.co.uk   T: 01225 314826
f/Boston Tea Party Cafes   /@btpcafes

7. SOCIETY CAFE

5 Kingsmead Square, Bath, BA1 2AB.

Housed in the corner plot of the beautiful listed buildings on Kingsmead Square is Society HQ. One of two outlets in Bath, this large and spacious cafe is a real find. Choosing the coffee roast is a team effort here, and the baristas often get together for cupping sessions at local roasters Round Hill. Two regularly changing espresso and two filter roasts are available, plus specials such as cold brew in the summer months. Serious about creating a cup to suit each customer, the team is friendly and knowledgeable. In summer the outside patio is perfect for people watching, while inside there are lots of seating options – from the sociable large tables, to a quirky basement nook where you can squirrel yourself away. A gallery of artworks and free Wi-Fi, plus attention from owners Adrian and Jane Campbell-Howard complete the experience.

KEY ROASTER
Round Hill

BREWING METHODS
AeroPress, Clever dripper, cold brew

MACHINE
La Marzocco FB80

GRINDER
Mahlkonig K30 x 2, Mahlkonig Tanzania, Mahlkonig EK43

OPENING HOURS
Mon-Fri 7am-6.30pm
Sat 7.30am-6.30pm
Sun 9am-6pm

INSIDERS TIP IMMERSE YOURSELF IN THE LARGE SELECTION OF QUALITY PHOTOGRAPHY BOOKS

www.society-cafe.com   T: 01225 442433

f/Society Cafe   🐦/@societycafebath

FLAT WHITE (SHORT) £2·10
(LONG) £2·20
AMERICANO £2·20
CAPPUCHINO £2·20
LATTE £2·30

TEA £2·00

HOT CHOCOLATE £2·50

SOMERSET & BRISTOL

TUNNOCK'S
MILK CHOCOLATE
TEA CAKES

CROCKER & WOODS
MAP.N⁰20 | PAGE.N⁰47

BRISTOL

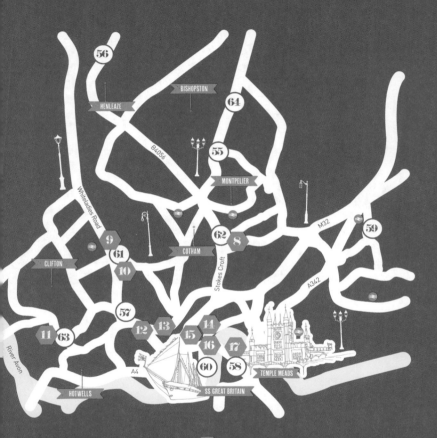

HENLEAZE

BISHOPSTON

56

64

55

B4056

MONTPELIER

Whiteladies Road

COTHAM

62

8

M32

59

CLIFTON

9

61

10

Stokes Croft

A362

57

11 63

12 13

14

15 16 17

River Avon

A4

60 58

TEMPLE MEADS

HOTWELLS

SS GREAT BRITAIN

COFFEE VENUE

3

MORE GOOD CUPS

8. THE BRISTOLIAN

2 Picton Street, Bristol, BS6 5QA.

A relaxed cafe by day and chic bistro by night, The Bristolian fits right in to the laid-back, bohemian style that Bristol is loved for. With a beautiful, listed exterior and a bright and colourful interior, there's a fabulously individual ambience to be found, whether you sit inside or out. Indulge in a bit of coffee chat with the friendly baristas as they prepare your Extract roasted coffee, or peruse the bookshelf before cosying up in a quiet corner with a good read. If you're feeling peckish, there's a fantastic breakfast menu featuring modern classics such as eggs florentine and belgian waffles. Then, as evening rolls in, share one of the huge tapas platters and a good bottle of red with friends – and of course the night wouldn't be complete without a top-notch after-dinner espresso.

INSIDERS TIP ASK FOR A "JAMES" COFFEE – OWNER JAMES' PERSONAL FAVE

KEY ROASTER
Extract

BREWING METHODS
Espresso

MACHINE
Sanremo

GRINDER
Sanremo

OPENING HOURS
Tues-Sat 8am-10.30pm
Sun-Mon 8am-5pm

www.thebristolian.co.uk T: 0117 9192808
f/The Bristolian Cafe 🐦/@bristoliancafe

MAP № 9. BRISTOL COFFEE HOUSE

121 Whiteladies Road, Clifton, Bristol, BS8 2PL.

This former Chandos Deli on Whiteladies Road has been transformed into a characterful coffee house and established itself as a popular local haunt for a quick bite or a gossip with friends. There's outdoor seating for an alfresco lunch, but it's worth sitting at one of the tables made from wooden crates to soak up the atmosphere. The cafe's urban, industrial vibe is pleasingly understated and really just a backdrop for the coffee and food, which rightly takes centre stage. The coffee bar offers a range of espresso-based drinks and at one end of the counter you'll find a selection of Chandos Deli salads, sandwiches and Italian pastries. The service is relaxed and friendly, and the staff knowledgeable about the beans used. As it's situated right next door to one of the big chains, it's a chance for Clifton's coffee lovers to support local and choose a more unique coffee experience.

KEY ROASTER
Wogan

Gluten FREE

BREWING METHODS
Espresso, pourover

COFFEE BEANS AVAILABLE

MACHINE
La Marzocco Linea

SOYA MILK AVAILABLE

GRINDER
Compak K10 RS
Barista Pro

WiFi

OPENING HOURS
Mon-Fri 7am-5pm
Sat 8am-6pm
Sun 9am-5pm

OUTDOOR seating

FAMILY friendly

INSIDERS TIP LOOK OUT FOR THE COFFEE INFUSED MEATBALLS

www.bristolcoffeehouse.co.uk   T: 0117 9706565

f/Bristol Coffee House   /@bristolcoffeehouse

MAP N° 10. BREW COFFEE CO

45 Whiteladies Road, Bristol, BS8 2LS.

For serious coffee knowledge, it's definitely worth making a beeline for Brew Coffee Co as owner Matt Atkins is passionate about spending time with his customers, passing on his favourite tasting notes and brewing methods at this unique, home-grown coffee shop. It's a great stop for lunch, with its counter of tasty quiches, frittatas and salads, and you can complement your food with the seasonal house coffee, specially selected through Clifton. *'We have a simple interior so we can focus our attention on what's important – the coffee, food and the service,'* explains Matt. However, it does have lots of Bristolian charm, with funky upcycled furniture including a slate bar made from old snooker tables. Broaden your coffee palate with the weekly-changing single origin filter coffee from a range of intriguing roasts – keep an eye on Brew's Facebook and Twitter pages for details.

KEY ROASTER
Clifton

BREWING METHODS
Filter

MACHINE
La Marzocco Linea

GRINDER
Mazzer

OPENING HOURS
Mon-Fri 8am-6pm
Sat 9am-6pm
Sun 10am-5pm

INSIDERS TIP NON COFFEE BREWS INCLUDE A MEAN LYCHEE, GINGER, CUCUMBER AND LIME JUICE, AND ALMOND MILK

www.Brew Coffee Company.co.uk   T: 0117 9732842

f/brewcoffeecompany   🐦/@brewcc

№11. SPICER+COLE

9 Princess Victoria Street, Clifton Village, Bristol, BS8 4BX.

When they relocated from the capital to Bristol, Carla and Chris Swift were quite surprised by how hard it was to find great coffee and food served in the same space – and so Spicer+Cole was born. Five years on, the West Country has caught up with the London coffee scene, and Spicer+Cole has gone from strength to strength too, opening its second venue in the centre of Clifton Village. The Cliftonites like to keep things local and Carla says, *'There's so much right on our doorstep, why not use it?'* The house blend is roasted by Bristol's Extract Coffee and there are also guest espressos to sample from the city's own Roasted Rituals and Little and Long. The counter is the hub of this light and spacious cafe, and it's laden with tempting pastries, cakes and tarts to accompany the coffee, while for lunch there's a good range of flatbreads, toasties and light dishes.

KEY ROASTER
Extract

BREWING METHODS
Espresso

MACHINE
Sanremo TCS

GRINDER
Sanremo

OPENING HOURS
Mon-Fri 7.30am-5.30pm
Sat-Sun 8.30am-5.30pm

INSIDERS TIP THE GLUTEN- AND DAIRY-FREE TUNISIAN ORANGE CAKE IS SO LOVED THAT ONE CUSTOMER EVEN WROTE A POEM ABOUT IT

www.spicerandcole.co.uk   T: 0117 9732485

f/Spicer and Cole   🐦/@spicerandcole

MAP №12. BOSTON TEA PARTY

75 Park Street, Bristol, BS1 5PF.

BTP Park Street was the first outlet in this small, family-owned independent cafe group, and is still its flagship store.

Opened in 1995, it's become a local institution for lovers of great coffee and rustic, homemade food, and is now one of five BTP cafes in Bristol (the others are in Clifton Village, Whiteladies Road, Gloucester Road and Stokes Croft). But lose any notions that this is a generic coffee chain, as each store has its own unique personality.

What unites them is the serving of simple, well-prepared food and drinks made with ethically sourced ingredients, and the result is feel-good coffee and food of excellent quality that's made from scratch onsite every day. It's been awarded three stars out of three by the Sustainable Restaurant Association too.

The Park Street branch is an urban retreat with lots of seating upstairs and a large tiered garden at the rear in which to enjoy a range of artisan coffees including the medium and dark house roasts, guest coffees and regularly changing filter coffee.

KEY ROASTER
Extract

BREWING METHODS
Espresso and filter

MACHINE
Nuova Simonelli

GRINDER
Mazzer Major

OPENING HOURS
Mon-Sat 7am-8pm
Sun 8am-7pm

INSIDERS TIP BUY FRESHLY ROASTED BEANS AND YOUR OWN BTP MUG INSTORE

www.bostonteaparty.co.uk   T: 0117 9298601

f/Boston Tea Party Cafes   /@btpcafes

№13. DIDN'T YOU DO WELL

20 Park Row, Bristol, BS1 5LJ.

A spot for those who are especially serious about coffee, Didn't You Do Well is the intriguingly named speciality coffee shop on Bristol's Park Row, down the hill from the university. Small, with minimal decoration and just a handful of simple tables and chairs, it's all about the bean here. The team takes great care with every serving, weighing and measuring to create caffeine perfection. The focus is mainly on single origin coffee and how origin, process, roast and brewing all affect flavour. A selection of

INSIDERS TIP TAKE A LOOK AT THE SLAYER ESPRESSO MACHINE – IT'S ONE OF ONLY A HANDFUL IN THE COUNTRY

roasters is used, including Clifton, Little and Long, and Has Bean, and a small selection of cakes and pastries is made daily for the cafe by local Hart's Bakery. The selection of loose-leaf teas from Waterloo Tea is an added attraction and it's a good spot to buy coffee-making supplies, too.

KEY ROASTER
Has Bean, Clifton, Little and Long

BREWING METHODS
Kalita wave, AeroPress, Clever dripper, syphon

MACHINE
Slayer

GRINDER
Modified Mahlkonig K30 Vario x 2 and a Mahlkonig Tanzania

OPENING HOURS
Mon-Fri 8.30am-4.30pm
Sat 9.30am-4.30pm

Gluten FREE

COFFEE BEANS AVAILABLE

SOYA MILK AVAILABLE

WIFI

CYCLE FRIENDLY

OUTDOOR seating

E: didntyoudowell@hotmail.com   T: 07807 416092

f/Didn't You Do Well   /@didntyoudowell

THE
PLACE
TO
GET
ALL
YOUR
COFFEE
GEAR

14. FULL COURT PRESS – SPECIALITY COFFEE

59 Broad Street, Bristol, BS1 2EJ.

The simple, pared-back surroundings at Full Court Press ensures nothing detracts from the coffee. It also means you'll get the full attention of owner Mat North, whose focus on the details is exemplary.

Mat is fluent in the science behind coffee (his background is in physics), but he also has an uncanny ability to identify and describe every flavour in his regularly changing single origin offerings.

Apart from a striking stained-glass window at the back of the shop and the La Marzocco machine, the main feature is two boards detailing the day's coffee offerings of two espresso and two filter options – with tasting notes.

'My aim is to present coffee in a more considered manner, treating it as a specialist ingredient,' says Mat. Food is also perfectly pared-back, with a small range of cakes, including gluten-free options and pastries from Bristol's Hart's Bakery. Mat is always sourcing artisan coffee, and his range of roasters include Tate, Round Hill, James Gourmet, Workshop, Nude, Square Mile, Clifton, Little and Long, Extract, Origin, Caravan, Notes and Drop Coffee.

KEY ROASTER
Multiple

BREWING METHODS
AeroPress, Clever dripper, syphon

MACHINE
La Marzocco Strada EP

GRINDER
Nuovo Simonelli Mythos 1 Climapro and Mahlkonig Vario-W

OPENING HOURS
Mon-Fri 7.30am-5pm
Sat 9am-5pm
Sun 10am-4pm

INSIDERS TIP ALL THE COFFEES ARE AVAILABLE AS TASTING SETS, SO YOU CAN TRY THE SAME COFFEE UP TO FOUR DIFFERENT WAYS

www.fcpcoffee.com   T: 07794 808552

f/Full Court Press – Speciality Coffee   ⅴ/@fcpcoffee

MAP № 15. SMALL STREET ESPRESSO

23 Small Street, Bristol, BS1 1DW.

Photo: Adam Gasson

Tucked away on a side street, this tiny espresso and brew bar is loved by in-the-know Bristolians, who make it their regular pit stop in the city for coffee pulled through the sky-blue La Marzocco. There's a rotating selection of guest espressos and filter coffee from top roasters including Square Mile, Nude and Extract, with useful tasting notes on the wall. Although the team here is serious about coffee, the vibe is cosy and friendly with rough hewn wood, bare brick walls and a good smattering of caffeinated reading.

INSIDERS TIP – ASK FOR A 'HIT AND GO' – A £3.50 HIT OF GUEST ESPRESSO WHILE YOU WAIT, WITH A FLAT WHITE OR PICCOLO TO GO. IT'S NOT ON THE MENU

Complement your beverage with freshly made sourdough sarnies and locally made treats such as salted caramel brownies from Bosh, and carrot cake from Hart's Bakery. Great for coffee to-go, there are also a few seats inside or you can perch on the handmade benches outside.

KEY ROASTER
Clifton

BREWING METHODS
Espresso, cold brew and AeroPress

MACHINE
La Marzocco FB-80

GRINDER
Mahlkonig K30s

OPENING HOURS
Mon-Fri 7:30am-4:30pm
Sat 9:30am-4:30pm

www.smallstreetespresso.co.uk
f/Small St. Espresso 🐦/@smallstespresso

16. PLAYGROUND COFFEE HOUSE

45 St Nicholas Street, Bristol, BS1 1TP.

Playground Coffee, which opened just a few months ago, aims to provide a unique experience, and certainly delivers on that promise – where else can you find Indian street pizza, artisan coffee, table football and more than a hundred card and board games? The inspiration came from co-owner Lily Drakoulakou's roots – back in Greece it's not unusual to spend all day at a cafe drinking coffee and playing games. Lily and her partner Fabian Dryden hoped to recreate that mood, along with the best possible coffee. There are up to four espressos on offer

INSIDERS TIP YOU CAN DRINK YOUR COFFEE WHILE SITTING ON A SWING, AN EXPERIENCE YOU WON'T FIND ANYWHERE ELSE

at any one time, including a blend created just for Playground by Andy Tucker at Clifton. *'It's zesty with orange citrus notes at the front and dark chocolate following through. It's an intricate cup,'* says Fabian. *'It's a very different approach to a house blend.'* The other espressos are rotating single origins and the team is currently experimenting to find a secondary house blend that'll work well with soya milk and sugar/syrup. The single origin filter coffees are well worth sampling too.

KEY ROASTER
Clifton,
James Gourmet,
Roasted Rituals

BREWING METHODS
AeroPress V60,
syphon, espresso

MACHINE
La Marzocco GB5

GRINDER
Mahlkonig K30 Twin,
2 x Mazzer Major E,
Mahlkonig Vario

OPENING HOURS
Mon-Fri 7.45am-6.30pm
Sat 9.30am-7pm
Sun 12pm-4.30pm

www.playgroundcoffee.co.uk   T: 0117 3290720

f/Playground Coffee House   /@playgroundcofco

MAP No. 17. CITY DELI

32 Victoria Street, Bristol, BS1 6BX.

It may only have opened in the spring of 2014, but City Deli in the heart of Bristol is proving a popular choice for a quick bite to eat and perfectly brewed coffee. This large, airy space has an industrial feel with long tables and bench seating filling the central area. The utilitarian décor is set off by shelves groaning with a colourful patchwork of drinks and gluten-free snacks. Service is quick and efficient, so it's great for those on a clock-watching break, but the spacious interior means you can find a quiet spot to while away the hours, and maybe catch up on some work. From the get-go, the plan for this family run cafe was to serve excellent coffee – and it does, working with Clifton to serve interesting batches of beans. Lunchtime bestsellers include jerk chicken, pulled pork and freshly made tortilla, alongside baguettes and panini fillings, which are fast becoming a local legend.

INSIDERS TIP WE LOVE THE CUTE MINIATURE MILK BOTTLES THAT ACCOMPANY THE COFFEE

KEY ROASTER
Clifton

BREWING METHODS
Espresso, drip

MACHINE
La Spaziale

GRINDER
Mazzer

OPENING HOURS
Mon-Fri 7am-6pm
Sat 9am-3pm

www.citydelibristol.co.uk   T: 0117 9250758

f/City Deli   🐦/@citydelibristol

MAP N° 18. TINCAN COFFEE CO

Major music festivals and events across the South West and UK.

As coffee vendors go, it doesn't get much cooler than Tincan Coffee Co's fleet of 1960s and '70s vintage trucks. Serving up quality espresso to festival goers, rugby fans and event attendees all over the South West, the Bristol-based company is revitalising the mobile coffee experience. Gone are the days when a tepid instant coffee was the only option at an outdoor occasion, now the guys at Tincan offer a different espresso blend from each of their four uniquely modified trucks. *'It's all about trying something a little different,'* says owner Adam White. He likes to use directly and exclusively traded blends whenever possible and, with single origin drip also on offer from guest roasters, there's a good chance you won't have tried a cup quite the same before. The Tincan trucks are also there to deliver tasty treats to hungry party goers, with smoothies, award winning cakes and artisan toasties on the menus.

KEY ROASTER
Clifton

BREWING METHODS
Espresso and
bulk brew drip

MACHINE
La Spaziale S5s

GRINDER
Mazzers

OPENING HOURS
Open as long as
the event is open

INSIDERS TIP LOOK OUT FOR A PERMANENT TINCAN SITE –
WITH A TWIST – IN THE FUTURE

---

www.tincanevents.com   T: 07725 880581

f/Tincan events   🐦/@tincanevents

MAP NO. 19. YEO VALLEY HQ

Rhodyate, Blagdon, Bristol, BS40 7YE.

S lightly off the beaten track, but with possibly the best view in the South West, is the restaurant and cafe at Yeo Valley HQ. At the foot of the Mendip Hills, it's a delightful slice of urban cool in a countryside setting.

You'd be forgiven for wondering why a company famous for its yoghurt and milk has a coffee shop, but then, Yeo Valley is not your run of the mill dairy – as a visit to its HQ testifies. This groovy space was once just the staff canteen, but now Yeo Valley's restaurant, Fodder, is open to the public. It's modern and stylish with some lovely surprises in the form of tongue-in-cheek furnishings and decoration. A selection of photos providing "reasons to be cheerful" line the corridor that leads to the restaurant and you'll spot different themed rooms on your visit – one's Victorian-style, another's an homage to the Beatles, and there are plenty of cow themed spaces too. The coffee is expertly presented, using beans from Mozzo, and there's a nice range of rustic, wholesome foodie options including a drop-dead gorgeous roast on Wednesdays.

KEY ROASTER
Mozzo

BREWING METHODS
Espresso and filter

MACHINE
S5 Compact ED
Group 2

GRINDER
Mazzer Lux

OPENING HOURS
Mon-Fri 8am-6pm

INSIDERS TIP TRY AN ESPRESSO SHOT POURED OVER A GENEROUS SCOOP OF YEO VALLEY'S ORGANIC VANILLA ICE CREAM

www.yeovalleyvenues.co.uk   T: 01761 463366

f/Yeo Valley   /@yeovalley

№20. CROCKER & WOODS

27 Catherine Hill, Frome, Somerset, BA11 1BY.

It's not often you find a place as memorable or with as much character as Crocker & Woods. It's in arty Frome and includes a gallery and industrial lighting shop alongside the coffee, which makes it a unique cafe experience. Single-handedly formed from the creative imagination of owner Chris Woodage (and his not-so-silent partner, Crocker the terrier), there's a bold and striking theme throughout that incorporates 1930s motorcycle culture and a splash of Mexican sunshine. It's not just the venue that Chris should feel proud of, as the coffee receives just as much care and attention. The house espresso, specially roasted by Round Hill, is ground to order and paired with non-homogenised milk to ensure a sweet flavour. Roasts vary throughout the year to reflect the changing seasons, and there are usually homemade cakes available for rumbling tums. Grab a place on one of the leather chesterfields and engage with Chris and the regulars in a bit of banter, or just relax and soak up the rough-around-the-edges authentic vibe.

KEY ROASTER
Round Hill

BREWING METHODS
AeroPress and espresso

MACHINE
La Spaziale S5

GRINDER
Mahlkonig K30

OPENING HOURS
Tues-Fri 9am-5pm
Sat 10am-5pm
First Sun of month
9am-4pm

Gluten FREE

COFFEE BEANS AVAILABLE

COFFEE COURSES AVAILABLE

OUTDOOR seating

INSIDERS TIP ASK CHRIS ABOUT HIS TIME ON THE ROAD WITH THE DEMON DROME WALL OF DEATH

www.crockerandwoods.com   T: 07773 766009

f/Crocker & Woods   🐦/@crockerwoods

MAP No 21. STRANGERS WITH COFFEE

31 St Cuthbert Street, Wells, Somerset, BA5 2AW.

There are not many baristas who reach the level of dedication achieved by Ivan Hewitt, so it's worth popping in to his coffee shop for a bit of caffeine-related chat. It's a very friendly and informal setting, where creating your perfect cup of coffee is the top priority: *'The best thing is seeing people's appreciation,'* says Ivan. A tea-drinking Yorkshireman, he became a coffee convert after visiting his son in Sydney. With his chef wife Susan, he first opened a cafe in Truro before moving to Wells to create his perfect coffee shop. It's simply and lightly decorated, with a little outside courtyard, and good food from Susan – often matched to the coffees. Ivan has trained with Origin and Allpress and takes every opportunity to develop his coffee knowledge; on a day off, he'll be out visiting top coffee spots. His enthusiasm and northern charm is infectious and has seen the shop develop a loyal local following. *'People who like good coffee come to us,'* Ivan says. *'They'll even cycle to us from outside the county.'* And if he is travelling and can't find a specialist coffee shop? *'I'll make do with a cup of tea.'*

INSIDERS TIP SUSAN'S MEDITERRANEAN FOOD CATERS FOR ALL DIETARY NEEDS AND IS MADE WITH HER CHICKENS' ORGANIC, FREE RANGE EGGS

KEY ROASTER
Allpress

BREWING METHODS
V60 pourover, syphon, AeroPress and cold brew

MACHINE
La Marzocco Linea

GRINDER
Mazzer Kony, Super Jolly, Vario

OPENING HOURS
Mon-Sat
8am-4.30pm
Sun occasionally
– check Facebook page

T: 07728 047233

f/Strangers With Coffee

MAP Nº 22. MR MILES TEAROOMS AND COFFEE SHOP

3-4 High Street, Taunton, Somerset, TA1 3PG.

There aren't many cafes where you can buy coffee roasted on site, but at Mr Miles Tearooms and Coffee Shop in Taunton you can do just that. It roasts its own coffee most days which *'creates a wonderful coffee aroma,'* says manager Colin Barrell. *'The freshness of the beans is paramount to get the best flavours.'*

It's the espresso that keeps the customers coming back to Mr Miles. It's a special blend that's been put together by the head roaster at the DJ Miles HQ in Porlock and customers can pick up a bag in the shop to take home, along with lots of other coffee paraphernalia. You can also enjoy a variety of cafetière coffees made with beans from around the world including Costa Rica, Colombian and Java – plus there's always a guest coffee being freshly ground.

This fully licensed tearoom is open for breakfast and lunch with temptations on offer, from the favourite Mr Miles rarebit (made to a secret recipe) to a range of 25 cakes made daily by the cafe's two bakers.

KEY ROASTER
DJ Miles

BREWING METHODS
Espresso and cafetiere

MACHINE
Rancillo

GRINDER
Fiorenzato and Mazzer

OPENING HOURS
Mon-Fri 8.30am-5pm
Sat 8.30am-6pm
Sun 9.30am-4pm

INSIDERS TIP SIGN UP FOR THE FRIENDS OF MR MILES CLUB FOR DISCOUNTS, SPECIAL OFFERS AND EVENTS

www.mr-miles.co.uk   T: 01823 322288

f/Mr Miles Tearooms   ✔/@timmrmiles

SOUTH COAST ROAST
MAP.Nº24 | PAGE.Nº52

23. CAFE BOSCANOVA

650 Christchurch Road, Boscombe, Dorset, BH1 4BP.

A pioneer of Bournemouth's growing coffee scene, Boscanova has been serving up speciality coffee and brewing single origins since 2007. It's easy to find in Boscombe district's pedestrianised shopping centre: spot the tree-canopied pavement tables and constant stream of customers through the door. Boscanova attracts a fiercely loyal bunch of locals of all ages, thanks to the barista team's mantra of "making coffee approachable". *'We're not special, we just know a lot about what we do,'* says head man Luke Lamb. A multi roaster cafe, the selection is based on what staff are into at any one time, so you can find artisan coffees coming from the USA and Scandinavia, along with own-bottled cold brew. The food offering covers porridge and granola and the best breakfast in Bournemouth (for veggies too), to personalised pancakes and fab lunches. Eclectic, a touch eccentric, colourful and with great music, you'll kick yourself if you leave Bournemouth without visiting.

INSIDERS TIP THE STAFF ARE TRUE AMBASSADORS FOR THE LOCAL AREA AND CAN RECOMMEND OTHER PLACES TO STOP IN AT - AND TRY THE PANCAKES TOO!

KEY ROASTER
Multiple

BREWING METHODS
Marco shuttle brewer

MACHINE
La Marzocco 3grp PID

GRINDER
Mazzer, manual, on demand

OPENING HOURS
Mon, Tues, Thurs and Fri 8am-4pm
Sat 8am-5pm
Sun 9am-4pm

Gluten FREE

COFFEE BEANS AVAILABLE

SOYA MILK AVAILABLE

WIFI

DISABLED ACCESS

COFFEE COURSES AVAILABLE

CYCLE FRIENDLY

OUTDOOR seating

FAMILY friendly

www.boscanova.com   T: 01202 395596

f/Cafe Boscanova   /@cafeboscanova

24. SOUTH COAST ROAST

24 Richmond Hill, Bournemouth, Dorset, BH2 6EJ.

Photo: Tom Powell

The little sister to Bournemouth coffee pioneer Boscanova, South Coast Roast is a serious coffee haven, right in the centre of town. It has all the character and laid-back charm of Boscanova, but in a more pared-back, geeky kind of way. It's where the Boscanova baristas train and a large, communal central table makes it a cupping paradise. Pop in, join in, or simply chill out and watch the shoppers go by. High ceilings, coffee sacks, LPs, artwork and bicycles – there's always something to catch the eye.

The simple menu of fast fresh food – prepared at Boscanova and carried over – completes a lovely coffee break experience. The team uses a variety of roasters from the UK and abroad, and serves espresso with milk and a roasting brew option, as well as a variety of single cup brews. Although it can get busy – especially at lunchtimes – it's a calming antidote to modern life, with smiling staff who always find time for coffee chat.

INSIDERS TIP TRY THE DIFFERENT VARIETIES OF COLD BREW, MADE AND BOTTLED IN-HOUSE

KEY ROASTER
Multiple

BREWING METHODS
Marco shuttle, Chemex, Clever french press, V60, cold brew, AeroPress

MACHINE
La Marzocco 2 grp

GRINDER
Anfim and Mazzer

OPENING HOURS
Mon-Fri 8am-5pm
Sat and Sun 10am-4pm

Gluten FREE

COFFEE BEANS AVAILABLE

SOYA MILK AVAILABLE

WIFI

DISABLED ACCESS

COFFEE COURSES AVAILABLE

CYCLE FRIENDLY

OUTDOOR SEATING

---

www.boscanova.com   T: 01202 551197

f/South Coast Roast

25. COFFEE SALOON

9 Haven Road, Canford Cliffs, Poole, Dorset, BH13 7LE.

This new coffee bar in Dorset has expansion plans in the pipeline – so it's one to keep an eye on. It's an inviting space: relaxed, cool and casual with, as the name suggests, a touch of the Wild West about it – there are even saddles hanging from the ceiling. It's a new venture for Colin Cross, the founder of The Dancing Goat in Poole and reflects Colin's creative touch – he has a background in design and retail – as well as his passion for coffee. This began in 1998 when the coffee bar he introduced into his homeware shop became an instant hit, and was further developed as a result of time spent in Australia. In the Saloon, he's used reclaimed materials in a stripped-back building and added cool music to create ambience. Also, unusually, there's no Wi-Fi. *'We like the idea that people can talk to one another,'* he says. The ethos is clearly also about creating a unique and exciting place to enjoy good coffee – created in collaboration with Origin, La Marzocco and a range of artisan coffees.

INSIDERS TIP DOGS ARE ALLOWED, AND THERE MAY EVEN BE SPACE FOR YOUR HORSE ...

KEY ROASTER
Origin

BREWING METHODS
Espresso

MACHINE
Linear PB5
La Marzocco

GRINDER
Mazzer Majors
Automatic

OPENING HOURS
Mon-Fri 7am-5pm
Sat 8am-5pm
Sun 9am-3pm

www.coffeesaloon.com   T: 07973 642466

f/Coffee Saloon   /coffeesaloon

MAP № 26. SOULSHINE

76 South Street, Bridport, Dorset, DT6 3NN.

The lucky people of Bridport have had a new hangout where excellent coffee is just one part of a funky package, since Soulshine opened in the spring of 2014.

An initial glance through its slightly Dickensian shop window reveals bookshelves displaying magazines, indy comics and graphic novels. There's a rustic wooden panelled serving counter and a menu blackboard – which covers the whole wall – decorated with butterflies. An arty feel pervades throughout, thanks to work from graffiti artist Xenz, right to the lovely little sunny courtyard, with its long wooden tables and white fence, painted with leaves and birds. Alongside the house espresso from Extract you'll find guest coffees on offer – including Amid Giants & Idols, Union, Origin and Square Mile. The team also creates an incredible range of juices and works to produce a fresh, healthy food offering (all breads baked in-house). You'll also want to pick up something from the deli.

KEY ROASTER
Extract

BREWING METHODS
Espresso

MACHINE
Sanremo Verona TCS

GRINDER
Mahlkonig K30 Vario AIR, Sanremo SR50

OPENING HOURS
Mon-Sat 9am-5pm
Sun 10am-4pm

INSIDERS TIP KIDS HAVE THEIR OWN SPECIAL PLAY AREA COMPLETE WITH VINTAGE FISHER PRICE TOYS – AND CHECK OUT THE MOOMIN MUGS

www.soulshinecafe.co.uk   T: 01308 422821
f/Soulshine Cafe   🐦/@soulshinecafe

27. AMID GIANTS & IDOLS

59 Silver Street, Lyme Regis, Dorset, DT7 3HR.

Just at the top of town, a little away from the crowd-filled streets around the historic harbour at Lyme Regis, sits the unusually titled Amid Giants & Idols, *'It's an anagram of my two nieces' names,'* explains owner Xanne Carey. It's a small independent coffee house and micro roaster, with UK Barista Championships semi finalist Xanne at the helm. Devoted to the art of coffee, it offers up to five seasonally selected coffees and a variety of brew methods. Roasting its own coffee using ethically sourced beans, the team also finds and promotes beans from new and up-and-coming local roasters. The overall vibe is homely and welcoming, with comfy basket and leather chairs and vintage memorabilia dotted around. Passionate about sharing a love of coffee, you'll find a friendly welcome no matter what your level of coffee expertise – and children are very welcome too. The level of care taken over the coffee also extends to hot chocolate and a range of fine loose-leaf teas. All this is combined with a gorgeous selection of locally made artisan cakes and chocolates.

INSIDERS TIP KIDS WILL LOVE THE ROCKING HORSE WHILE GROWN UPS ENJOY THE WIFI

KEY ROASTER
Amid Giants & Idols

BREWING METHODS
Espresso, drippers, AeroPress, cold brew

MACHINE
Marzocco Linea

GRINDER
Various Mazzers

OPENING HOURS
Mon-Sun 10am to 4pm or 5pm
Please check website

www.amidgiantsandidols.com   T: 07928 790254
f/Amid Giants & Idols   ￼/@AmidGiantsIdols

THE EXPLODING BAKERY
MAP.№33 | PAGE.№64

EXETER

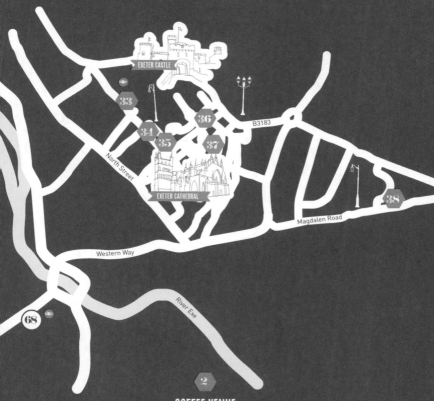

EXETER CASTLE

33

36

B3183

34

35

37

North Street

EXETER CATHEDRAL

38

Magdalen Road

Western Way

River Exe

68

2

COFFEE VENUE

3

MORE GOOD CUPS

≋28. BROOM WAGON COFFEE

3 Cross Street, Seaton, Devon, EX12 2LH.

While owner Glenn Moorley is an enthusiastic cyclist – and the name (after the van that traditionally picks up riders that abandon during a Grand Tour) and interior suggest a two-wheeled theme – you don't need to be a fan of Lycra to immerse yourself in the vibrant scene at this East Devon coffee shop. Broom Wagon is an up-and-coming destination for coffee buffs, with locally produced Coffee Factory espresso being pulled through the La Marzocco Linea machine. You'll also find guest single origins being explored through various brew methods, as Glenn experiments with the AeroPress and V60. The cafe's location makes it the perfect pit stop after a walk (or ride) along the Jurassic Coast, and it also welcomes those too young for coffee and four-legged friends. Refuel with one of the intriguing handmade tray bakes, with changing flavour combinations from blueberry bakewell to almond and fig. In warm weather, enjoy the beach vibe and cool down with a refreshing iced coffee from the AeroPress.

KEY ROASTER
Coffee Factory

BREWING METHODS
AeroPress, V60

MACHINE
La Marzocco Linea
Classic EE, 2 group

GRINDER
Mahlkonig K30 Vario,
Mazzer Super Jolly
Electronic,
Baratza Virtuoso

OPENING HOURS
Tues-Fri 9.30am-4pm
Sat 10am-4pm
Sun 10am-2pm

Gluten FREE

WiFi

CYCLE FRIENDLY

OUTDOOR seating

FAMILY FRIENDLY

INSIDERS TIP COFFEE IS SERVED WITH MEASUREMENTS OF 3, 5 AND 7OZ OF MILK – AND MAKE SURE YOU ASK ABOUT NEARNAKEDMAN

www.cafebroomwagon.com   T: 07747 105918

f/Broom Wagon Coffee   /@cafebroomwagon

№29. IVAN'S COFFEE

At events and festivals across the South West.

After years of touring as a roadie around the world with bands such as Ben Howard and Mumford and Sons, Ivan Bunyard was tired of drinking bad coffee, so he decided to share his passion for a good brew with the world. Ivan and his wife Deby work from a lovingly restored 1962 Volkswagen Splitscreen van, which they've owned for 12 years. It's seen its fair share of festivals and surf trips, and now dispenses speciality coffee to-go. Expect friendly, relaxed service to complement great coffee that's made with love, and a fantastic range of snacks including Mrs Gill's Country Cakes and Teoni's Cookies. Look out for coffees from Ivan's travels too, including Bun from Australia and New Zealand, and Stumptown from America.

KEY ROASTER
Crediton

BREWING METHODS
Espresso, drip filter and cold brew

MACHINE
Fracino retro lever with dual fuel

GRINDER
Fracino C3r

OPENING HOURS
On request

INSIDERS TIP THE QUIRKY STYLE OF IVAN'S COFFEE REFLECTS HIS TRAVELS. IF YOU'RE LUCKY YOU MIGHT GET A ROCK AND ROLL TALE WHILE IVAN MAKES YOU A MEAN FLAT WHITE

www.ivans-coffee.com   T: 07796 128057

f/Ivans Coffee   ▼/@ivanscoffee

№30. BOSTON TEA PARTY
21-22 Tuly Street, Barnstaple, Devon, EX31 1DH.

The North Devon branch of this small, family-owned independent cafe group, BTP Barnstaple is the go-to place in the town for quality coffee.

Situated in a big ol' former wool mill, it's at the heart of the community and has established itself as a cultural hub with an enviable track record of showcasing diverse and talented artists, from comedy and theatre to art and poetry.

The team ethically sources a range of artisan coffees and there are two roasts as standard: the dark roast with its flavour profile of cocoa, liquorice and toasted nuts, and the medium roast which is all about chocolate, hazelnut and marmalade. The filter coffee changes monthly.

While the coffee is much loved, the homemade food's a draw too – from big breakfast pancakes with maple syrup and bacon to healthy superfood salads and a wide range of freshly made sarnies and soups. Awarded a Sustainable Restaurant Association three star (out of three) rating.

KEY ROASTER
Extract

BREWING METHODS
Espresso and filter

MACHINE
La Marzocco

GRINDER
Mazzer Major

OPENING HOURS
Mon-Sat 8am-6pm
Sun 9.30am-5pm

INSIDERS TIP IN SUMMER, JOIN NORTH DEVON'S COFFEE AFICIONADOS CONGREGATING ON THE FRENCH STYLE CAFE TABLES IN THE SUN

www.bostonteaparty.co.uk   T: 01271 329070
f/Boston Tea Party Cafes   ⦿/@btpcafes

MAP №31. WILD THYME CAFE

5 Caen Field Shopping Centre, Braunton, Devon, EX33 1EE.

INSIDERS TIP CHECK OUT THE WALL MURAL BY LOCAL ILLUSTRATOR EMILY HAMILTON

There's a definite fusion of surfer serenity and coffee nerdiness to be found at Wild Thyme Cafe. With internationally inspired dishes and chai teas served alongside speciality coffee, this family of travel lovers has certainly put its own stamp on Braunton's busy little shopping hub. The North Devon coffee shop is serious about serving up a good cup of coffee, sending all of its baristas for training with the chaps at Origin and ensuring ultimate freshness by grinding to order. This friendly cafe has an eclectic clientele, offering something for everyone. Try a homemade smoothie or a green juice, and there's also a fab breakfast and lunch menu available. The venue is licensed and hosts a variety of themed evenings with live music and great food, enjoyed by locals and holidaymakers alike. You can also book Wild Thyme's event catering service – which includes unbeatable hog roasts.

KEY ROASTER
Origin

BREWING METHODS
Espresso

MACHINE
Astoria

GRINDER
Mazzer Super Jolly Timer

OPENING HOURS
Mon-Sun 9am-4pm
Extended hours in summer months

www.wildthymecafe.co.uk   T: 01271 815191

f/Wild Thyme Cafe

№32. CREDITON COFFEE COMPANY

1 Market Square House, Market Street, Crediton, Devon, EX17 2BN.

It's not often you find a cafe where you can watch the coffee being roasted while sipping a freshly brewed cup made from beans roasted in-house – so this is a rather special place to visit. The family run coffee shop has a contemporary and spacious interior, but the true character of the Webbs' working roastery shows through in the bags of green beans lining the glass-fronted exterior and with the noise and smell of the Diedrich roaster at work. With at least six different roasts of its own coffee to choose from, and a range of brewing methods at son Dan Webb's brewing bar, coffee geeks can go wild with flavours here. They've converted the locals too, sparking an interest in quality coffee in the small community and developing their customers' appreciation of the speciality bean by taking the time to chat about their passion. Regulars come flooding back to try the seasonally changing espresso and to pick up a couple of bags of roasted beans to take home.

KEY ROASTER
Crediton

BREWING METHODS
Espresso, filter, drip filter, AeroPress, Chemex and syphon

MACHINE
Fracino Retro

GRINDER
Ditting and Mahlkonig

OPENING HOURS
Mon-Sat 9am-5pm

INSIDERS TIP CAROLE'S HOMEMADE CAKES ARE A MUST, ESPECIALLY THE FAMILY FAVE: HONEY AND BUTTER FLAPJACKS

www.creditoncoffee.co.uk   T: 01363 775065

f/Crediton Coffee Company   🐦/@creditoncoffee

№33. THE EXPLODING BAKERY

1B Central Station Buildings, Queen Street, Exeter, Devon, EX4 3SB.

It's the smell that will lead you to The Exploding Bakery, one of Exeter's favourite coffee haunts. This is primarily a bakehouse, so the warmth of industrial ovens and wafts of home cooking spill out onto the paved area outside, drawing customers from the train station entrance a few yards away. It was a natural step for coffee-loving baker and co-owner Oli Coysh to have his own onsite machine – and to apply the same level of care to the brew served as he does to his cakes. Monmouth is the house coffee, but there's a second grinder for various guest coffees, including Clifton, Round Hill, Square Mile and Climpson & Sons. He also uses "proper" milk: organic and non-homogenised from local dairy, Ashclyst Farm.

Oli specialises in tray bakes cakes for coffee shops and his creations are matched to speciality coffee. *'We use a little less sugar and concentrate on the actual flavour of the cake, with the intention of not overpowering your drink,'* he says. Cosy up inside, grab a table on the pavement or take your coffee to-go.

KEY ROASTER
Monmouth

BREWING METHODS
Espresso, V60 dripper, AeroPress

MACHINE
La Marzocco Linea 2 Group

GRINDER
Mazzer Super Jolly x 2

OPENING HOURS
Mon-Fri 8am-4pm
Sat 9am-4pm

INSIDERS TIP TRY A MONMOUTH FLAT WHITE WITH A GLUTEN-FREE ALMOND BROWNIE – A PERFECT FLAVOUR PROFILE MATCH

---

www.explodingbakery.com   T: 01392 427900

f/The Exploding Bakery   ✔/@explodingbakery

34. DEVON COFFEE

88 Queen Street, Exeter, Devon, EX4 3RP.

Devon Coffee has a reputation as a small coffee shop with a big personality, where you'll find "good coffee, well made by nice people". Set right in the heart of Exeter city centre, it could be easily missed at first glance, but this tiny wooden panelled store is a must-visit.

Owners Steve and Kim Pearson started their mission to provide quality artisan coffee to the people of Devon ten years ago when Steve, a former coach builder, made his own custom converted van. Following the coffee van's success, the Queen Street cafe opened its doors in 2012 and has been serving speciality coffee and simple food ever since. There's cosy seating inside or you can perch at a couple of little tables out on the pavement. Keep an eye on Kim and Steve (a UK semi finalist in the 2014 UK Barista Championships) as they're currently working on a project to roast their own beans in-house from a custom built coffee roaster.

INSIDERS TIP WHEN THE SHOP WAS REFURBISHED THEY DISCOVERED AN 1873 ABSTINENCE POSTER STUCK TO AN OLD PANELLED WALL

KEY ROASTER
Origin

BREWING METHODS
Espresso, V60,
Clever dripper

MACHINE
La Marzocco

GRINDER
Mahlkonig K30

OPENING HOURS
Mon-Sat 8am-6pm
Sun 10am-4pm

www.devoncoffee.co.uk   T: 07795 105250
f/Devon Coffee   ✔/@coffeedevon

№35. BOSTON TEA PARTY

84 Queen Street, Exeter, Devon, EX4 3RP.

BTP Exeter is a hidden gem in the city. From the small downstairs area you'd never guess that one floor above there's a huge dining room that feeds and waters a community of local foodies who are also passionate about great coffee.

Eclectically furnished with quirky mix and match chairs and tables and local artwork, it prides itself on serving simple well-prepared food and drinks made with great ingredients.

Sustainably sourced, affordable and feel-good are key here and everything is made in-house each day. It's not surprising to learn that it's been awarded three stars (out of three) by the Sustainable Restaurant Association. Popular with those who like breakfast at any time of day, it serves them from dawn to dusk.

A few miles away is BTP Honiton, a sort of elegant English tearoom with the added buzz of an urban cafe – very much in keeping with the town itself. Both offer a range of artisan coffees including house dark and medium roasts and monthly changing filter coffees.

KEY ROASTER
Extract

BREWING METHODS
Espresso and filter

MACHINE
Nuova Simonelli

GRINDER
Mazzer Major

OPENING HOURS
Mon-Sat 7am-6pm
Sun 8am-6pm

INSIDERS TIP CHECK OUT THE COUNTER THAT'S GROANING WITH HOMEMADE CAKES, BAKES AND PASTRIES. WE LOVE THE PASTEIS DE NATA

www.bostonteaparty.co.uk T: 01392 201181
f/Boston Tea Party Cafes /@btpcafes

36. ARTIGIANO ESPRESSO BAR

248 High Street, Exeter, Devon, EX4 3PZ.

A relative newcomer to Exeter's coffee scene, Artigiano is unusual in that while it looks like a high street chain, it's actually far from it.

Right in the heart of the city's shopping area, it has instant appeal with big glass windows, masses of space and a delectable array of salads, sandwiches, pastries and cakes. And usually, on a sunny day, you'll also find lots of people sipping coffee outside at its tables. Once inside, it's easy to spot how serious the team here is about coffee: the baristas (headed by Matt Woolley) have their own stand-alone counter and their recipe for the perfect shot is up on the board. A seasonal range of hand-picked beans from some of the world's best high-altitude single estate farms (which changes monthly) complements the house blend, which is roasted exclusively for Artigiano.

INSIDERS TIP BARISTA MATT REPRESENTED THE UK IN THE 2014 WORLD LATTE ART CHAMPIONSHIPS

Another plus is the extended opening hours, which means you can pop in for beautifully crafted coffee after work or in the evening – before sampling one of its boutique wines, craft beers or cocktails.

KEY ROASTER
Origin

BREWING METHODS
Espresso

MACHINE
La Marzocco Linea PB

GRINDER
Mazzer Major

OPENING HOURS
Mon-Wed 7.30am-8pm
Thurs-Fri 7.30am-11.30pm
Sat 8am-11.30pm
Sun 10am-6pm

Gluten FREE

COFFEE BEANS AVAILABLE

SOYA MILK AVAILABLE

WIFI

DISABLED ACCESS

CYCLE FRIENDLY

OUTDOOR SEATING

FAMILY FRIENDLY

www.artigiano.uk.com   T: 01392 499169

f/Artigiano Espresso & Wine Bar Exeter   ✔/@artigianoexeter

Nº 37. CHANDOS DELI

1 Roman Walk, Exeter, Devon, EX1 1GN.

Modern and spacious, this deli on the edge of Exeter's Princesshay shopping area serves great coffee from Bristol-based Wogan Coffee, alongside a tempting spread of foodie treats – both to eat in and take away.

The Exeter Chandos is one of a small group of long-standing independent delis originating in Bristol and, like its sister stores, is run by a dedicated and friendly team, with specialists dedicated to different foods and drinks. There's an excellent selection of continental and local cheeses, antipasti and meats, as well as the carefully considered range of wines, ciders and beers. When it comes to coffee, an impressive effort is made to create the perfect cup for each customer, and the team has regular training, both in-house and with Wogan, with some of

KEY ROASTER
Wogan

BREWING METHODS
Espresso

MACHINE
Rancillo

GRINDER
Mazzer

OPENING HOURS
Mon-Sat 9am-6pm
Sun 10am-4pm

INSIDERS TIP THE MUCH LOVED CHORIZO SAUSAGE ROLLS ARE MADE ON SITE EVERY DAY - BUT THEY SELL OUT QUICKLY!

the guys also gaining extra individual qualifications in areas such as latte art. One of the nicest things about this Chandos is its location alongside the old Roman city wall. It's a peaceful spot, but also close to the shopping centre so is popular with day trippers and shoppers, as well as Exeter's foodies and office workers.

www.chandosdeli.com T: 01392 437379
f/Chandos Deli Exeter /@chandosdeli

38. DARKHORSE ESPRESSO

135 Magdalen Road, Exeter, Devon, EX2 4TN.

After living in Canada and the US for two decades, Neil and Sarah Bunting have brought their love of coffee and coffee shop hospitality back home, setting up a friendly, community-based cafe in a leafy suburb of Exeter, where coffee lovers, children and even pooches are warmly welcomed. Expect something a little eclectic and arty, as they've transformed this former DIY shop into a modern cafe with simple but unusual furniture and fittings. Striking blackboard walls list the daily offerings, while an embossed

INSIDERS TIP JOIN IN ONE OF THE VIBRANT COFFEE CUPPING EVENTS, OR CHILL OUT IN THE LITTLE OUTDOOR COURTYARD

tin ceiling – imported from the US – is a stunner. The coffee counter is the hub of the operation, and a good selection of blends and single origins are available, served via a manual La Marzocco, or as a V60 or Chemex drip. If you feel peckish, there are breakfast and lunch options, from granola and homemade muffins to organic soups and cakes – with beans and brewing equipment also available to purchase.

KEY ROASTER
Clifton, Ozone

BREWING METHODS
Espresso, V60 and Chemex

MACHINE
La Marzocco Linear

GRINDER
Mazzers

OPENING HOURS
Mon-Fri 8am-4pm
Sat 10am-3pm

www.darkhorseespresso.co.uk　T: 07825 397663

f/Darkhorse Espresso UK　🐦/@darkhorse135

№39. HANNAHS SEALE-HAYNE

Howton Lane, Newton Abbot, Devon, TQ12 6NQ.

'*Life's too short for bad coffee,*' says Sam Miller, who heads the catering operation at Hannahs – an unusual bistro set in a striking Edwardian building. This buzzing venture at the heart of the Seale-Hayne complex, near Newton Abbot, is run by local charity the Dame Hannah Rogers Trust, which helps children and adults with disabilities. Set in 90 acres of spectacular Devon countryside, it's in a sheltered quadrangle courtyard with suntrap alfresco seating. Inside, there's split level seating, including large comfy sofas, in wood-panelled rooms.

The site also has shops and a gallery in addition to its activity areas for outdoor pursuits, music, and the recording studio. The Bistro is fast becoming a foodie destination in its own right, with a range of Mediterranean-influenced dishes. However, good food starts with good coffee, according to Sam, who checks the quality of her barista team's coffee every day. '*So much care is taken in the growing and roasting of coffee,*' she says. '*We owe it to the people who've produced it to serve an excellent drink – I want us to lead the way.*'

KEY ROASTER
Origin

BREWING METHODS
Espresso

MACHINE
Sanremo

GRINDER
Sanremo

OPENING HOURS
Mon-Sat 8am-9pm
Sun 9am-9pm

INSIDERS TIP PROBABLY THE ONLY PLACE IN THE SOUTH WEST WHERE YOU'LL FIND A COFFEE ROBOT – HE'S CALLED RUAIRDAN

Gluten FREE

SOYA MILK AVAILABLE

WIFI

DISABLED ACCESS

CYCLE FRIENDLY

OUTDOOR seating

FAMILY FRIENDLY

www.discoverhannahs.org   T: 01626 325800

f/DiscoverHannahs   /@discoverhannahs

40. TANGERINE TREE CAFE

50 High Street, Totnes, Devon, TQ9 5SQ.

Sipping an artisan coffee in the peaceful walled garden of the Tangerine Tree Cafe, you can relax knowing you're doing your bit for the local environment, because this place has a brilliant home-grown ethos. Owners Ness and Martin Turner pride themselves on supporting local suppliers and reducing their carbon footprint, while offering an entirely homemade breakfast and lunch menu. A prominent feature on Totnes' famously independent High Street, this family friendly cafe provides a single origin from El Salvador – the El Majahual region – as well as loose leaf teas and Luscombe's organic fruit juices.

INSIDERS TIP THE WALLED GARDEN IS ESPECIALLY LOVELY FIRST THING ON A SUMMER'S MORNING

The quiet second floor, away from the busy street and dotted with comfy lounge chairs, is the perfect spot to appreciate the great coffee or lose yourself in a book. Or if you want to be social, there's nothing like a bit of bonding over a brew and delicious cakes from the cafe's sister company Totnes BakeHouse. Well-behaved dogs are allowed, and it's licensed.

KEY ROASTER
Clifton

BREWING METHODS
Espresso

MACHINE
Cimbali

GRINDER
Mazzer Super Jolly

OPENING HOURS
Tues-Sat 8.30am-5pm

www.tangerinetree.co.uk   T: 01803 840853

f/Tangerine Tree Cafe

41. COASTERS COFFEE COMPANY

Unit 1, Abbots Quay, Prince of Wales Road, Kingsbridge, Devon, TQ7 1DY.

A spot of people watching goes hand in hand with a passion for good coffee shops, and Coasters Coffee Company is a great place to indulge in both. With a spacious, modern interior and comfy chairs, this speciality coffee shop in a quiet corner of the South Hams is a favourite with locals and tourists alike. There's a changing guest espresso and filter coffee, often featuring local roasters such as Origin and Extract, with a custom house blend from Clifton always available as the go-to cup. For the home enthusiast, a range of brewing equipment and coffee are available for purchase, from an AeroPress to various beans used in-store. With a range of homemade paninis and sandwiches on offer at lunchtime and cracking cakes from Devon favourites, Exploding Bakery and Peck & Strong, Coasters isn't just a coffee hang out, it's a vibrant meeting place for all walks of life.

INSIDERS TIP CHECK OUT THE BOOKCASE FILLED WITH GAMES AND BOOKS – AND BOOK SWAP IF YOU CAN'T PUT IT DOWN!

KEY ROASTER
Clifton

BREWING METHODS
Espresso and
Clever dripper

MACHINE
La Marzocco Linea

GRINDER
Mahlkonig K30 Vario,
Mazzer Super Jolly
x 2, Baratza Filter

OPENING HOURS
Mon-Fri 8.30am-
6pm
Sat 8.30am-5pm

T: 01548 853004

f/Coasters Coffee Company ／@coasterscoffee

Drinks
Gear
Knowledge

Beyond the Bean, the Bristol based producers of Sweetbird and Zuma, are proud supporters of the South West Coffee Guide

t: 0117 953 3522
@beyondthebean
w: beyondthebean.com
e: info@beyondthebean.com

CORNWALL

THE BREW HOUSE
MAP.№50 | PAGE.№83

№42. LIBERTY COFFEE

4 Northgate Street, Launceston, Cornwall, PL15 8BD.

The first thing you'll notice about this Launceston coffee shop is owner Ben Statton's utter enthusiasm and excitement about coffee. Using a wide range of artisan South West roasters, Liberty Coffee's ethos is to introduce its visitors to the many fascinating and changing flavours the bean has to offer.

Just around the corner from the High Street, the cafe's menu is short and sweet with black, white or filter, with the coffee origins and tasting notes available to browse on the board. But don't fret if you haven't swotted up on the jargon, the baristas are more than happy to fill in any gaps in your coffee knowledge. It's not just a place for serious chat either, with a light and airy décor you can simply relax with a good brew and soak up the chilled ambience. For something a little different, try one of the real hot chocolates made from single origin cocoa.

INSIDERS TIP EXPERTLY BAKED CAKES, MADE ON THE PREMISES, ARE AS SPECIAL AS THE COFFEE – WE RECOMMEND THE BAKEWELL TART

KEY ROASTER
Square Mile, Workshop, Clifton, Origin, Round Hill

BREWING METHODS
AeroPress, V60 dripper, Chemex

MACHINE
La Marzocco Linea

GRINDER
Mazzer Major Electronic x 2, Mahlkonig Vario, Nuova Simonelli Mythos One

OPENING HOURS
Mon-Fri 9am-5.30pm
Sat 9am-5pm

www.liberty-coffee.co.uk   T: 01566 773223

f/Liberty Coffee   🐦/@libcoffee

№43. WOODS CAFE

Callywith Cottage, Cardinham Woods, Bodmin, Cornwall, PL30 4AL.

You wouldn't be mad to think you'd stepped into a fairytale as you approach the charming Woods Cafe in Cardinham Woods. Deep within 650 acres of woodland, this cottage cafe is the pinnacle of traditional country style, with a roaring fire in winter and homemade floral curtains framing the windows. A popular retreat for visitors heading off on the surrounding mountain bike and walking trails, this family run eatery prides itself on using fresh and local ingredients, especially when it comes to the coffee served. With its own signature blend – The Beast of Bodmin – delicately created by Hands-On in Wadebridge, visitors are in for a unique coffee experience in the Cornish countryside. And complement your coffee or Cornish-grown Tregothnan tea with a slice of homemade cake; regulars love it so much that owner David says, *'If we stopped making the beloved bakes, there'd be an uproar.'*

KEY ROASTER
Hands-On

BREWING METHODS
Espresso

MACHINE
Sanremo

GRINDER
Sanremo

OPENING HOURS
10.30am-4.30pm
364 days a year.
Closed on
Christmas Day.

INSIDERS TIP THERE ARE ALWAYS A COUPLE OF GLUTEN-FREE CAKES AVAILABLE – ESPECIALLY GOOD ARE THE CHOC BROWNIES

www.woodscafecornwall.co.uk　T: 01208 78111

f/Woods Cafe　🐦/@woodscafekernow

№44. RELISH FOOD & DRINK

Foundry Court, Wadebridge, Cornwall, PL27 7QN.

It's a pretty safe bet you'll experience one of those perfect coffee moments as you sit in the sunny courtyard outside this little Cornish gem.

On every coffee fan's list of must-visit places, Relish Food and Drink is a cafe and deli in the heart of the north Cornwall town of Wadebridge. Its secret weapon is owner Hugo Hercod, UK barista champion of 2008 (the same year he came tenth in the world championships). The cafe is just yards from the busy shopping area and it's a peaceful little haven. Freshly ground beans from Cornwall's leading roaster, Origin, are given specialist treatment by Hugo and his small team – which includes 2014 UK barista championship finalist Mark Williams.

The interior is simply decorated with fresh green and white walls, slate floors, comfy sofas and wooden chairs and tables. An added bonus is the deli next door, also owned by Hugo, which is packed full of the best Cornish products – along with some fabulous foods from further afield – and of course you get to try some of the deli pickings in the cafe. As with the coffee, this is quality fare and you can pop in for breakfast, lunch and afternoon tea.

KEY ROASTER
Origin

BREWING METHODS
Espresso and filter

MACHINE
Astoria Plus4U
2 group

GRINDER
Mazzer Robur E

OPENING HOURS
Mon-Sat 9am-4pm
Sun 9am-5pm
(Sundays in summer months only)

INSIDERS TIP ALL MILK BASED DRINKS ARE MADE WITH LOCAL MILK FROM TREWITHEN DAIRY IN LOSTWITHIEL

www.relishfoodanddrink.co.uk   T: 01208 814214

f/Relish Food & Drink   🐦/@relishcornwall

45. STRONG ADOLFO'S

Hawksfield, A39, Wadebridge, Cornwall, PL27 7LR.

Strong Adolfo's isn't your typical roadside cafe. Situated just off the A39 near Wadebridge, it's a striking wooden building with panoramic glass windows and inside, the stripped-back interior has a clean, industrial feel.

At the heart of Strong Adolfo's is Mathilda, originally from Sweden, and her husband John who has lived in Cornwall since the age of 12.

Mathilda brought the Swedish tradition of "fika" – coffee with something sweet to accompany it – to the cafe. And this is certainly a great spot for fika, with speciality coffee sourced from Origin and a daily selection of delicious homemade cakes. It's a great place to stop for breakfast or lunch too, with influences taken from around the world.

INSIDERS TIP JOHN'S SIDE PROJECT OF CUSTOMISING MOTORCYCLES AND SHAPING SURFBOARDS ADDS A UNIQUE FLAVOUR TO THE CAFE

KEY ROASTER
Origin

BREWING METHODS
Espresso and Clever dripper

MACHINE
La Marzocco

GRINDER
Mazzer

OPENING HOURS
Mon-Fri 8.30am-5pm
Sat-Sun 9am-5pm
Check website for winter opening hours.
Evening openings for special events

www.strongadolfos.com   T: 01208 816949
f/Strong Adolfo's   🐦/@strongadolfos

MP.№ 46. 108 COFFEE HOUSE

108c Kenwyn Street, Truro, Cornwall, TR1 3DJ.

You may be used to having wine or pizza delivered to your door, but it's not often you find a coffee shop offering local delivery. Proving to be extremely popular with Truro businesses, 108 Coffee is supplying artisan coffee to the masses via text, Twitter and email ordering. It's not just cappuccinos and lattes that fly out the door – the "grab and go" lunch, freshly made each day in the cafe, is also a hit with the city's workforce and busy shoppers, who regularly make a quick stop for a tasty bite to eat. If you don't want to live life in the fast lane,108 Coffee's HQ

INSIDERS TIP THE TEAM BREWS ON CORNWALL'S ONLY LA MARZOCCO STRADA

is a light and relaxing space with plenty of furniture to sink into, and families and four-legged friends are welcome too. Highly trained baristas serve quality coffee with constantly changing roasts sourced from a range of artisan producers.

KEY ROASTER
Origin

BREWING METHODS
Espresso,
Hario V60

MACHINE
La Marzocco Strada
MP 3 Group

GRINDER
Mazzer Robur,
Mahlkonig Tanzania

OPENING HOURS
Mon-Fri 7am-6pm
Sat 8am-6pm

www.108coffee.co.uk   T: 07582 339636

f/108 Coffee House   🐦/@108_coffee

47. GOOD VIBES CAFE

28 Killigrew Street, Falmouth, Cornwall, TR11 3PN.

I f you enjoy a quality coffee paired with fantastically fresh and wholesome food, look no further than Good Vibes Cafe in Falmouth. A result of the creative and culture-packed imaginations of John Hersey and Hannah Rutland, it certainly meets their brief of creating a relaxed meeting and eating place that serves delicious, hearty food. Sustainably produced local ingredients are used in inspiring breakfasts, Sunday brunches and lunch menus that change so often you're bound to discover something new each time you visit. The artisan coffee alternates just as frequently, and a range of roasters keeps the three grinders packed with the best seasonal blends and guest espressos. Don't be downhearted if your old favourite isn't here upon return, because John likes to try new and inventive blends. *'The wackier the better!'* he says.

KEY ROASTER
Origin

BREWING METHODS
Espresso

MACHINE
La Marzocco Linea
3 Group

GRINDER
Malkonig K30 x 2,
Mazzer Luigi
Super Jolly

OPENING HOURS
Mon-Sat 8.30am-
5.30pm
Sun 10am-2pm

INSIDERS TIP TRY THE SIGNATURE SANDWICH OF FRESHLY POUNDED GUACAMOLE, CREAMY HUMMUS AND HOT SMOKED STREAKY BACON WITH A BLAST OF SMOKED PAPRIKA

T: 01326 211870

f/Good Vibes Cafe　🐦/@good_vibes_cafe

№48. ESPRESSINI

39 Killigrew Street, Falmouth, Cornwall, TR11 3PW.

Photos: Owen Stratton www.owenstratton.co.uk

Falmouth's Espressini opened in 2011 and is well worth a visit. In three short years it's become one of the venues at the forefront of Cornwall's burgeoning cafe scene. Its seasonal espresso selection offers something for every palate, with beans sourced from the best speciality roasters in the UK, as well as occasional international guests. A choice of single origin filters is also available, brewed using Clever dripper, AeroPress and various other pourover methods. Owner Rupert Ellis and his team were listed in *The Independent*'s Top 50 speciality coffee shops in the UK, and last year, manager Hannah Giles was named top female barista in Cornwall, so your caffeine fix is in good hands. With the addition of the Espressini Kitchen in June 2014, it's not just all about the coffee either; breakfast is an all-day affair, while lunch happily lingers on into the afternoon.

INSIDERS TIP MAKE A DATE FOR BREAKFAST AND GET YOUR ORDER IN FOR EGGS BENEDICT

KEY ROASTER
Multiple

BREWING METHODS
Kalita PO,
Clever dripper,
vacuum, AeroPress

MACHINE
Nuova Simonellli
Aurelia 2G

GRINDER
Mazzer Royal,
Mahlkonig, Bunn,
EK43

OPENING HOURS
Mon-Sat 8am-
5.30pm
Sun 9.30am-4pm

Gluten FREE

COFFEE BEANS AVAILABLE

SOYA MILK AVAILABLE

WIFI

DISABLED ACCESS

COFFEE COURSES AVAILABLE

OUTDOOR seating

FAMILY FRiendly

www.espressini.co.uk   T: 07580 590248
f/Espressini   ✔/@espressini39

MAP № 49. THE YELLOW CANARY CAFE

12 Fore Street, St Ives, Cornwall, TR26 1AB.

Walking along the cobbled streets of surfy St Ives, it's hard to miss The Yellow Canary's vibrant yellow sign swinging in the breeze. Three generations of the Haase family have worked hard to uphold the popular reputation of this family run coffee shop. Locals love the choice of speciality coffee served with homemade biscotti, and the family sources top quality local produce for its delicious food offering. Cornish roaster Origin provides the beans, which usually change season by season, but owner Paul loves to hear what his customers think and often changes the blend according to the desires of the regulars. Although it was first established in 1972, it's kept pace with the times and the interior has a contemporary, natural theme throughout – with splashes of that cheerful canary yellow. A bakery down the road supplies bread for a range of tasty sandwiches, of which it's the house favourite – chorizo, goat's cheese and red onion chilli jam ciabatta – that keeps the regulars flocking back.

INSIDERS TIP IT'S KNOWN LOCALLY AS THE ST IVES VERSION OF US TV SITCOM, CHEERS

KEY ROASTER
Origin

BREWING METHODS
Espresso and AeroPress

MACHINE
La Marzocco

GRINDER
Mazzer Major E

OPENING HOURS
7 days a week
March - November
Summer 7am-10pm
Winter 9am-5pm

COFFEE BEANS AVAILABLE

SOYA MILK AVAILABLE

www.theyellowcanary.com T: 01736 797118

f/The Yellow Canary Cafe /@yellowcanarycaf

MAP N° 50. THE BREW HOUSE

Harbour Head, Porthleven, Cornwall, TR13 9JA.

In the lovely little fishing village of Porthleven, The Brew House is Origin Coffee Roaster's own flagship coffee shop. It's where you'll find head barista Will Pitts and his team experimenting with various brews and roasts. Central to Will's extensive and continually evolving menu are single estate coffees, roasted down the road at Origin HQ and rotated according to the season. These include micro-lot coffees that have been sourced exclusively for The Brew House on Origin's direct trade trips.

The menu also has specials such as affogato with salted caramel ice cream. Overlooking the harbour, The Brew House has a stunning interior thanks to designer Anna Hart, who has created a laid-back space which makes full use of the sea view. Also on offer are home brewing courses, run by Will, which'll teach you the art of filter brewing and the science behind extraction, using a variety of apparatus and filter materials.

INSIDERS TIP EXPERIENCE THE WORLD OF ORIGIN COLD BREW FIRST HAND

KEY ROASTER
Origin

BREWING METHODS
AeroPress, V60, Chemex, AltoAir, cold brew

MACHINE
La Marzocco Linea PB

GRINDER
Mazzer Major E Grinders x 2, Mazzer Super Jolly Grinder

OPENING HOURS
Mon-Sun 9am-5pm
Easter to October half term and December 20-January 3

COFFEE BEANS AVAILABLE

SOYA MILK AVAILABLE

COFFEE COURSES AVAILABLE

OUTDOOR seating

---

www.origincoffee.co.uk/the-brew-house   T: 01326 574337

f/The Brew House Porthleven   /@thebrewhouse1

MORE GOOD CUPS

51. THE ROOKERY

35 Marlborough Street, Faringdon,
Oxfordshire, SN7 7JL.

therookeryshop@gmail.com

T: 01367 242030

f/The Rookery - Beautiful Things 🐦/@therookeryoxon

52. JIKA JIKA

4 Brunel Square, Bath, BA1 1SX.

www.jikajika.co.uk

T: 01225 469253

f/Jika Jika 🐦/@jika_jika

53. THE GREEN ROCKET

1 Pierrepont Street, Bath, BA1 1NY.

www.thegreenrocket.co.uk

T: 01225 420084

f/The Green Rocket Cafe 🐦/@greenrocketcafe

54. CHANDOS DELI BATH

12 George Street, Bath, BA1 2EH.

www.chandosdeli.com

T: 01225 314418

f/Chandos Deli 🐦/@chandosdeli

55. BAKERS AND CO

193 Gloucester Road, Bristol, BS7 8BG.

www.bakersbristol.co.uk

E: contactbakersandco@gmail.com

f/Bakers and Co Bristol 🐦/@bakersandco

56. CHANDOS DELI BRISTOL

97 Henleaze Road, Bristol, BS9 4JP.

www.chandosdeli.com

T: 0117 9074391

f/Chandos Deli 🐦/@chandosdeli

57. FRISKA QUEEN'S ROAD

70 Queen's Road, Clifton, Bristol, BS8 1QU.

www.friskafood.com

T: 0117 9300989

f/Friska 🐦/@friskafood

58. FRISKA VICTORIA STREET

36 Victoria Street, Bristol, BS1 6BY.

www.friskafood.com

T: 0117 9298971

f/Friska 🐦/@friskafood

59. NO.12 EASTON

12 High Street, Easton, Bristol, BS5 6DL.

www.12easton.com

T: 07824 664003

f/No12 Easton 🐦/@no12easton

60. SPICER+COLE

1 Queen Square Avenue, Bristol, BS1 4JA.

www.spicerandcole.co.uk

T: 0117 9220513

f/Spicer and Cole 🐦/@spicerandcole

61. BOSTON TEA PARTY

97 Whiteladies Road, Bristol, BS8 2NT.

www.bostonteaparty.co.uk

T: 0117 9239571

f/Boston Tea Party Cafes   /@btpcafes

62. BOSTON TEA PARTY

156 Cheltenham Road, Bristol, BS6 5RL.

www.bostonteaparty.co.uk

T: 0117 3291454

f/Boston Tea Party Cafes   /@btpcafes

63. BOSTON TEA PARTY

1 Princess Victoria Street, Bristol, BS8 4HR.

www.bostonteaparty.co.uk

T: 0117 9730338

f/Boston Tea Party Cafes   /@btpcafes

64. BOSTON TEA PARTY

293 Gloucester Road, Bristol, BS7 8PE.

www.bostonteaparty.co.uk

T: 0117 9424654

f/Boston Tea Party Cafes   /@btpcafes

65. THE DANCING GOAT

31 Parr Street, Poole, Dorset, BH14 0JX.

www.thedancinggoat.co.uk

T: 07973 642466

f/The Dancing Goat   /@thedancinggoat1

66. NUMBER 35 COFFEE HOUSE & KITCHEN

35 High West Street, Dorchester, Dorset, DT1 1UP.

www.coffeehouseandkitchen.com

T: 01305 549269

f/Number 35 Coffee House & Kitchen
/@No35CoffeeHouse

67. BOSTON TEA PARTY

Monkton House, 53 High Street, Honiton, Devon, EX14 1PW.

www.bostonteaparty.co.uk

T: 01404 548739

f/Boston Tea Party Cafes   /@btpcafes

68. CAFE AT 36

36 Cowick Street, Exeter, Devon, EX4 1AW.

www.cafeat36.co.uk

T: 01392 410352

f/Cafe at 36   /@cafeat36

69. TUBESTATION POLZEATH

Trebetherick Hill, Polzeath, Cornwall, PL27 6TB.

www.tubestation.org

T: 01208 869200

f/Tubestation Polzeath   /@tubestationcrew

70. GYLLY BEACH CAFE

Cliff Road, Falmouth, Cornwall, TR11 4PA.

www.gyllybeach.com

T: 01326 312884

f/Gylly Beach Cafe   /@gyllybeachcafe

71. PICNIC CORNWALL

14 Church Street, Falmouth, Cornwall, TR11 3DR.

www.picniccornwall.co.uk

T: 01326 211655

f/Picnic Cornwall   /@picniccornwall

72. HUB ST IVES

4 The Wharf, St Ives, Cornwall, TR26 1LF.

www.hub-stives.co.uk

T: 01736 799099

f/Hub   /@hubstives

COFFEE NOTES HAILING FROM CANCALE IN BRITTANY, DAISY HAS A CULINARY BACKGROUND AND WORKED IN MICHELIN-STARRED RESTAURANTS BEFORE ARRIVING IN BRISTOL, AGED JUST 19. INSPIRED BY MEETING "PASSIONATE COFFEE PIONEERS" SHE BECAME A FREELANCE COFFEE TRAINER AND CONSULTANT AND STARTED COFFEA ARABICA OVER A DECADE AGO. DAISY HAS BEEN WORKING WITH THE LONDON SCHOOL OF COFFEE FOR SEVEN YEARS, UNION HAND ROASTED FOR 12 YEARS AND MANY OTHER LEADING COMPANIES IN THE INDUSTRY. SHE ALSO OPENED LEAZE FARM COFFEE SCHOOL IN BRISTOL IN 2008.

THE ART OF
THE BARISTA

Daisy Rollo of Coffea Arabica is passionate about where speciality coffee comes from, how it's grown and how it's served. Every year she travels to coffee plantations to meet coffee farmers, often documenting their work in film and through photography. Back in the UK, she works as a freelance coffee trainer and runs courses from her coffee school in Bristol.

'I visit plantations around the world and spend time with farmers and pickers to understand the work involved in delivering some of the best speciality coffee. My role as a trainer is to make sure I pass on this information to the barista to help them understand the origin of the product and how to get the best out of it,' she says.

What qualities does she think is required to become an excellent barista? *'Above all else, the barista must be passionate about coffee, as their role is to deliver and showcase not just the product, but also the love and care taken by all the people involved in the coffee chain – from the farmers and pickers who have grown, harvested and processed the coffee, to the roaster who has developed the perfect roast profile in order to enhance the characteristics of the coffee. Extracting coffee can be done using different brewing methods, from an espresso machine to a syphon, all of which involve a methodical approach, a fine-tuned palate, an understanding of the recipes and a respect for the product,'* she says.

'I VISIT PLANTATIONS AROUND THE WORLD AND SPEND TIME WITH FARMERS AND PICKERS TO UNDERSTAND THE WORK INVOLVED IN DELIVERING THE BEST SPECIALITY COFFEE.'

What about beyond the pure understanding of coffee flavours? *'Customer service skills are also important. A good barista should be friendly, welcoming and recognise their regular customers. Baristas need to be able to work in a very busy environment – it is essential they are organised, good at multi-tasking and have great communication skills,'* says Daisy. *'I believe a great barista is able to deliver quality and consistency with a great personality.'*

www.coffeaarabica.co.uk　T: 07766 533157

f/daisyrollocoffeaarabica　🐦/@daisyrollo

BREWING UP
HISTORY

THE SOUTH WEST'S RELATIONSHIP WITH COFFEE GOES BACK TO A TIME WHEN NOT EVERYONE WAS EXACTLY THRILLED ABOUT IT ...

In 1674, an anonymous pamphlet called *The Women's Petition Against Coffee* warned that coffee led menfolk *'to trifle away their time, scald their chops, and spend their money, all for a little base, black, thick, nasty, bitter, stinking, nauseous, puddle water'*.

Without doubt, coffee has the power to inspire some passionate feelings – both for and against – but once England's first coffee shop had opened, reportedly in Oxford in 1650, there was no looking back.

Coffee houses became places for intellectual debate, where gentlemen would meet to discuss the politics of the day, and they were also popular hangouts for artists – so in many ways not much has changed.

There was a rumour that Mol's Coffee House in Exeter was the first in England – although it's since proved untrue. But the striking building, at No 1 Cathedral Close was used as a coffee house during the 18th century, originally leased by a Mary Wildy and run by a succession of women for the next 100 years or so. There's also reference to a "coffy roome" in Truro in the late 17th century, kept by "stationer" John Weekes – the stationery was probably news-sheets kept for customers to read.

Often linked to the temperance movement, coffee shops were created to try and draw

people away from pubs. The Plymouth Coffee House Company opened The Borough Arms in Bedford Street in 1878. It sounded very much like a pub, but the gentlemen of Plymouth would find no alcohol there. They must have loved the beautiful furnishings though – there were marble tables, comfy chairs, plenty of newspapers to read and coffee, tea and cocoa urns supplying refreshments on every floor.

The company also produced its own coins, which, like vouchers, were used to try and draw people in. Plymouth's coffee links may even go back to the Mayflower, which apparently set sail from the quay for America in 1620 carrying a wooden pestle and mortar which was later used to make "coffee powder".

With its seafaring past and miles of coastline, there are many tales of coffee reaching English shores via the South West. Coffee was aboard the ship Albemarle which was wrecked off the coast near Polperro in Cornwall in December 1708, and there are accounts of coffee being smuggled in by way of the Dorset coast between 1716 and the mid 1730s.

Being such a key trading port there's no doubting the significance of Bristol in the story of coffee. In the 1700s the Corn Street area was the place to find a good coffee shop. The city's business district, it was filled with merchants hanging out, drinking coffee and trading in goods landing ashore from slave trade areas like North America and the Caribbean.

Coffee shops were places to hear the news, and items from pamphlets and newspapers were read aloud to the coffee drinkers. Cafe Revival, in a three story listed building at 56 Corn Street, lays claim to being the site of the city's oldest coffee shop, with coffee being served on the spot since the mid 1600s. A Cooke's Coffee house was mentioned in a will referring to the site in 1713 and in 1723 it became the London Coffee House. Many years later in the 1930s it became the home to the famous Carwardines – which had its own onsite roastery.

The last five years have seen a huge revival in the South West's coffee scene. Back in 1674, The Women's Petition stated in no uncertain terms that *'our countrymen's palates are become as fanatical as their brains'*, and *'the continual sipping of this pitiful drink is enough to bewitch'*. They'd probably say the same today ...

'TRIFLE AWAY THEIR TIME, SCALD THEIR CHOPS, AND SPEND THEIR MONEY, ALL FOR A LITTLE BASE, BLACK, THICK, NASTY, BITTER, STINKING NAUSEOUS PUDDLE WATER'.

Article refs: H L Douch, *Old Cornish Inns and Their Place in the Social History of Cornwall*; Todd Gray, *Exeter Unveiled*; Roger Guttridge, www.burtonbradstock.org.uk/smuggling; www.plymouthherald.co.uk; www.bristolpost.co.uk; Barbara Wells Sarudy, 18C American Women blog and thanks to Angela Broome, librarian archivist, Courtney Library, Truro

ROASTING COFFEE IN 1881

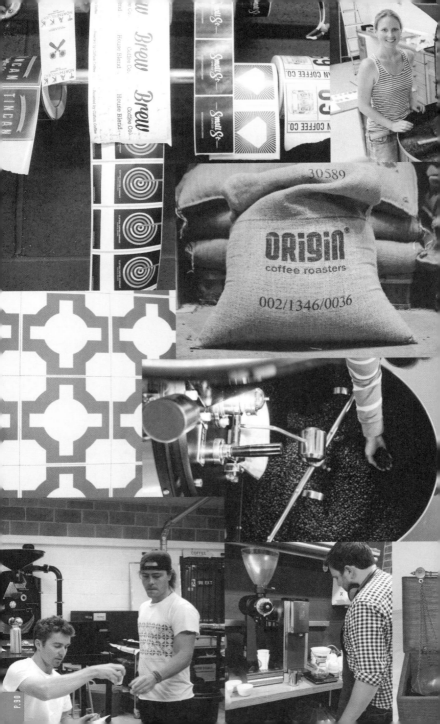

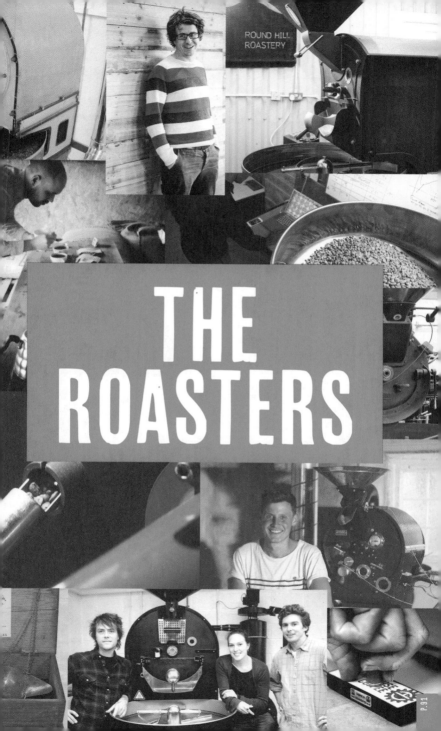

THE
ROASTERS

ANDY
TUCKER

A TOAST
TO THE ROASTERS

Up until about five years ago, you could count the number of coffee roasters in the South West on one hand. Today we find ourselves among a plethora of some of the country's finest roasters – all right here in our backyard – and I'm very proud to be a part of it.

We felt it important that the *South West Independent Coffee Guide* should not only share with readers where to drink amazing coffee in our region, but also to introduce them to who provides those amazing coffees, and what those businesses in turn bring to the coffee scene.

'EACH ROASTER INCLUDED IN THIS GUIDE HAS ITS OWN PERSONALITY, ITS OWN PHILOSOPHY ON ROASTING'

We all have differing opinions about what makes the perfect cup of coffee, and each roaster included in this guide has its own personality, its own philosophy on roasting, and varying ideas on what its contribution should be to the process of preparing an amazing cup of coffee.

Nevertheless, all of the businesses featured share a common appreciation for great coffee, and we're proud to have selected those we feel represent the South West in its truest light.

Andy Tucker
Head of coffee, Clifton Coffee Roasters

🐦 /@cliftoncoffee

73. ROASTWORKS COFFEE CO

www.roastworks.co.uk   T: **01404 891332**

f/Roastworks Coffee Co   /@roastworksdevon

'When I was young I used to get so frustrated when I was carted around to my parents' friends' houses and all they'd talk about was coffee.'

Will Little's childhood was a tad unusual. As the child of two artisan roasters, he grew up surrounded by coffee sacks and beans. His parents were at the forefront of the Second Wave in artisan coffee, starting roasting coffee in Finland in the late 1980s before moving to Devon to set up Little's Speciality Coffee. Probably due to a surfeit of coffee talk, Will initially decided not to do "the coffee thing" and instead became a graphic designer. But, surrounded by the emerging new coffee scene when he was working in London, he became inspired by the work of roasters like Monmouth and Square Mile. Returning to the West Country, Will and his wife Caroline joined the Little's team, but also saw the need for a new type of roastery, one based on the Third Wave coffee revival – and Roastworks Coffee Co was born.

'What always intrigued me about coffee when I was a child was that it came from so far away,' says Will. 'I was fascinated by these exotic bags with their colourful printed designs. It's still the case that most people don't know much about how their coffee is grown and who grows it. But I can go to a farm in Mexico and get coffee from a certain part of that farm and the grower can tell me exactly why it tastes like it does. If that farmer is growing an amazing coffee with its own intrinsic flavour and character, then it's our job to highlight those characteristics, by using science and art in the roasting.'

Making speciality coffee accessible is also part of the Roastworks ethos. 'There are some great coffee shops out there, but I'm not seeing the transference of quality coffee into the home,' says Will. 'That's what we want to change, and it's why we're so focused on the retail sector. We want people to be able to get the best quality coffee when they go shopping.'

www.dustyape.com   T: 01225 753838

f /Dusty Ape   🐦 /@dustyape

AVAILABLE
ONLINE

Discovering a shared love of good coffee and culinary flavours – while watching a footie match – was what first united Dusty Ape's founders, Phil Buckley and Evan Metz.

The pair pooled their considerable experience in the coffee and real ale industries to form Wiltshire's only small-batch coffee roaster. Using a traditional gas-fired roaster, they've crafted an exceptional range of single estates, single origins and signature blends.

Phil and Evan take a taste-led approach to sourcing and roasting coffee. *'Coffee roasting, like brewing ale, requires a methodical approach, attention to detail and skill in identifying and combining flavours,'* says Evan. Initially, the chaps started home roasting, spending months researching the London coffee scene before developing their own unique identity. *'We want to turn people on to decent coffee,'* says Phil. *'To savour, think about, discuss, share and enjoy it – without*

being overly prescriptive about how it should be drunk. Great coffee needs to be accessible. Before we buy, we taste top grade, seasonal coffees from importers who actively support coffee growers. We select premium coffees with distinctive tastes that we think people would like to try. Back at the roastery, Evan and I then develop tailored roast profiles for each bean through sample roasts and repeated cupping until we get the flavour and balance right.'

'You have to train your palate to coffee's subtle array of flavours,' adds Evan, *'which can only be done by roasting and tasting, again, again and again. For us, coffee is about relationships first and foremost: as people's tastes evolve and their understanding and coffee knowledge deepens we provide advice, skills and equipment to help them explore all its possibilities.'*

MAP № 75. ROASTED RITUALS COFFEE

www.roastedritualscoffee.com   T: 0117 2440098

f/Roasted Rituals Coffee   /@roastedrituals

Monday morning can be a struggle for most of us, but it's not post-party recovery or workday blues that affect the team at Roasted Rituals. Their week starts with "cupping" an industry term for coffee tasting. *'It's a ritual we adhere to,'* says Tahi Grant-Sturgis. *'We cup every day, and every roast, to ensure our palate remains sharp, and we know how our coffee is tasting.'*

Tahi was a barista in New Zealand for many years before moving to the UK and working for an independent roaster in Glasgow. With her husband Patrick, she set up Roasted Rituals in 2013, and began by exploring the coffee regions.

'It was easy to convince Patrick to get involved, he has a great palate and, being a Devon boy with an agricultural management degree, travelling and building strong relationships with coffee farmers is something he particularly enjoys.'

The company took a major step forward earlier this year when it was joined by roaster Courtney Taylor Jackson, a New Zealander who worked for the acclaimed roastery Seven Seeds in Melbourne before moving to the UK.

'Courtney comes with an enormous wealth of coffee knowledge,' says Tahi. *'Not just in roasting, but his understanding of brewing makes him invaluable to the training and workshops we offer. It's also vital we understand the importance of brewing for ourselves, and how it affects the perception of taste.'*

It's this knowledge and attention to detail, that demonstrates the company's commitment to quality ethos. There's an adventurous spirit at Roasted Rituals, which is shared by all three team members, along with a determination to raise the bar in terms of quality and expectation.

'Coffee changes a lot,' says Courtney. *'We can easily forget that it's a fruit and so at the mercy of any number of variables which will change its character from season to season. We want to really embrace these changes and showcase the differences, not just keep trying to replicate the same product. The aim is to open people's eyes to the quality of coffee - to push boundaries.'*

76. OWEN'S COFFEE ROASTERS

MAP No 76.

www.owenscoffee.com   T: 0800 8799791

f/Owens Coffee   /@owenscoffee

AVAILABLE ONLINE

Everyone in the small team at Owen's loves coffee and shares the passion of owner and chief roaster Lorraine Bridden. Plymouth-born Lorraine bought the business about four years ago, coming to the artisan coffee scene from a science background. It's this scientific approach that's given her the necessary skills of persistence, dedication and attention to detail that being a roaster demands. She uses a Toper roaster to develop bright, fresh and uplifting roasts and and is helped by a small team of incredibly dedicated caffeine lovers, who all come from backgrounds in coffee or hospitality.

If you're looking for a caring roaster, then Owen's pretty much ticks all the boxes. For a start it's 100 per cent organic and Fairtrade, and Lorraine is extremely careful about sourcing beans, understanding how they're grown and supporting small scale growers.

Back home, at the base in deepest Devon, the team works hard to develop local connections, both with suppliers and by supporting local cafes and coffee shops. Even the coffee branding, which reflects the surrounding beautiful countryside, uses the work of local artist Maggie Smith.

The team is careful about where Owen's coffee is served and would rather expand the business slowly, developing the all-important relationships with restaurant and cafe owners. *'We want to have our coffee in places that are passionate about it and who serve it well,'* says Lorraine. *'We don't just regard ourselves as coffee suppliers, but rather key partners in their business with the aim of mutual success.'*

This very personal, friendly approach is ingrained in the business, and you could say is reflected in the largely female make up of the team. *'Coffee roasting is very sensory,'* says Lorraine, *'and involves a great attention to detail, which I suppose is quite a feminine trait. It's probably why we're so meticulous with every aspect of our work.'*

MAP № 77. LITTLE & LONG

www.littleandlong.com   T: 07956 638669

f/Little and Long Coffee Roasters   ✔/@littleandlongcc

AVAILABLE ONLINE

'You've been roasting all day, you're hot and tired, but then you get to that point when the beans start to change colour and there's this wonderful smell ...'
Saskia Falconer, founder of Bristol-based Little and Long, is clearly in love with the roasting process. Describing the transformation of the hard bean as the heat draws out the moisture, changing it from green to yellow to brown, she says, 'You have to keep looking and adjusting. If it's not quite right it won't taste any good, and it will also be different depending on the day's weather and humidity.'

Saskia's long association with coffee began when she was growing up in New Zealand, where supermarkets would stock aisles of different coffees, 'all with the roasting dates on them', continuing when she spent time working with two roasters in Italy. 'In Italy, coffee is steeped in tradition, rules and regulations. It's a very strict industry – but they were both doing something different. They taught me that coffee is not a static thing.'

After her year studying in Italy, Saskia, who's also a physiotherapist, returned to Exeter and started roasting at home, supplying beans to friends and from an occasional market stall. Then, after an intense year with a roaster in Cape Town, she returned to Bristol where the roasting took over full time and Little and Long began. She loves to take her beans to market and can be found at Temple Quay. 'I love the interaction with people,' she says. Caring passionately about the people who work in the coffee industry, she's acutely aware of the chain involved in farming the product. She also wants her coffee to have broad appeal. 'I just want people to have a good cup of coffee. I'm just as satisfied having ten customers who say they had a really nice cup of coffee than one who says, "wow that's amazing, I've never tasted strawberries before!". Good coffee shouldn't be an exception, it should be the norm.'

NO. 78. ROUND HILL ROASTERY

www.roundhillroastery.com   T: **01761 435888**

f/Round Hill Roastery   ✐/@roundhillcoffee

AVAILABLE ONLINE

ddie Twitchett remembers first falling in love with coffee. *'It was a naturally processed Ethiopian Shakiso coffee which tasted like strawberries. It was unbelievable, so totally different and super exciting.'*

Eddie set up Round Hill Roastery in a rented warehouse space near Bath two and a half years ago. He was just 23. He now regularly roasts up to half a tonne a week, but despite the increased workload (and in such a short amount of time), he's never lost his intense passion and excitement for coffee.

Much of his inspiration comes from Colonna & Small's in Bath. Eddie's frequent visits to the coffee shop resulted in him persuading the shop's owner and award winning barista, Maxwell Colonna-Dashwood to give him some training. It wasn't long before Eddie had also enrolled at the London School of Coffee.

He's always been driven, and at the age of 16 he'd already set up his own business selling cakes and sandwiches. Completing a business-focused degree gave him the

acumen to start seriously investigating his own food focused company, but there was never any doubt it would be coffee.

'What I get most excited by has always been food and drink because I'm fascinated by tasting things,' he says. *'I'd worked in food and met lots of successful chefs – all enthusiastic and passionate people. There's something very contagious about being around them.'*

He's also never forgotten the incredible customer experience he had at Colonna & Small's, and the way he was introduced to a world of new flavours. It's this instinctive feeling and excitement for coffee, along with a desire to share that feeling, that gives Round Hill its energy and individuality.

'It's the interaction I love, the conversations about flavour that keep me obsessed. I enjoy talking to customers – whether they're wholesale clients or people passing by at a farmers' market. It's how I got into it and I think it'll always be what inspires me.'

№79. COFFEE FACTORY

AVAILABLE ONLINE

www.thecoffeefactory.co.uk   T: 01297 551259

f/Coffee Factory   ✈/@coffee_factory

To truly achieve a great coffee you need a true artisan – which is where Coffee Factory's Danny Parfitt comes in. He's been in the speciality coffee world for some time – both as a barista and roaster. In fact by 2006, after returning home following a spell working in Australia, he was already competing in the UK Barista Championships. By 2007 he had opened a cafe in Axminster with his partner, Justine Hutchings, and the roasting soon followed.

'We've always wanted to give our customers the best quality coffee and create our own blends, so it made sense to start roasting,' says Danny. The Coffee Factory soon grew and by 2012 roasting had taken over completely. They sold the cafe and moved to new premises in the Devon countryside which is where you'll now find Danny and Justine and their team hard at work, sourcing, cupping, roasting and tweaking to unlock the best flavours and personality of every coffee coming through the factory.

The coffee is of speciality grade and, working with Falcon, Coffee Factory has now bagged its first world-exclusive micro-lot – quite an achievement for a small-scale roaster. Coffee from an area of orange bourbon trees on the Finca Bosque Lya farm in El Salvador will be picked exclusively for Coffee Factory's customers – some of whom are celebrity chefs.

You can buy beans online and there's a strong wholesale side to the business too. Danny and Justine have crafted a great selection of seasonal blends for their customers, alongside a choice of single origins which make for great guest coffees. They also sell a range of brewing equipment and machinery.

Danny has a background as a chef and his culinary skills and palate have given him a good foundation. As well as the tasting, he loves the theatre of roasting – something that's inspired the company's direction. There's already an on-site tasting/training room, and an open invitation for people to pop in and sample coffees, particularly on cupping days.

№80. AMID GIANTS & IDOLS

www.amidgiantsandidols.co.uk   T: 07928 790254

f/Amid Giants & Idols   🐦/@amidgiantsidols

AVAILABLE
ONLINE

Former teacher Xanne Carey never really fancied coffee – until she visited New Zealand and Australia. One trip to the land of speciality coffee and she was hooked.

She returned to England and when the opportunity came up to have her own coffee place, she jumped at the chance and set up base in Lyme Regis. Initially the focus was on brewing great speciality coffee and her newly acquired barista skills led to her achieving 11th place in last year's UK Barista Championships.

Xanne's always been fully committed to finding beans that are ethically sourced, but it was her desire to understand the full process of coffee production which sparked an interest in roasting.

'About two years ago we found a vintage roaster in an old fashioned general store in Devon. It had fallen out of operation and so we lovingly restored it and added some modern technology to bring it back into use,' she says.

The cast iron 1930s Viennese Swadlo roaster takes pride of place in the roastery and is used exclusively to roast all of its seasonally selected speciality grade green beans, which are sourced from across the globe.

In part due to her teaching background, Xanne enjoys passing on her knowledge to customers. She runs classes, helping people understand how the process works – from bean to brew.

Amid Giants & Idols is very much a small-scale micro roastery and it's keen to link up with coffee houses, customers, importers and other roasters who share the same passion. Xanne provides one to one training for new clients and she loves sharing her barista skills and coffee knowledge. *'Coffee, its provenance, its quality, its producers and a sustainable future for the farmers are what matters,'* she says. *'There's a growing network of roasters and coffee houses working together across the South West to share our knowledge and help customers appreciate what's important in the production and brewing of coffee. Most of all, I thrive on seeing people getting excited by speciality coffee – that's what we're here for.'*

MAP № 81. ORIGIN COFFEE

www.origincoffee.co.uk   T: **01326 574337**

f /Origin Coffee Roasters   /@origincoffee

Cornwall-based Origin Coffee is one of the country's leading speciality coffee roasters and its owner, Tom Sobey, has certainly earned his position among coffee royalty.

This is a company that goes the distance and, in its efforts to provide the very best seasonally grown coffee, it deliberately set out on a mission to source its beans direct. Tom says, *'We believe that seasonal coffee traded directly is the best way to ensure an exceptional product. So we visit the farms and mills we work with (or do so through our trusted partners) and reward them for producing the best quality crops through sustainable and ethical practices. This creates a shared commitment to both quality and equality, and encourages continued crop development and innovation.'*

Tom's team is constantly on the hunt for exclusive, highly prized lots, which are then offered as monthly single origins. Beans are roasted in Cornwall, using a Loring Smart

Roast – the world's first environmentally friendly coffee roaster – and craftsmen roasters take care to roast lightly, enhancing the natural characteristics of the coffee.

Origin features in many of the country's top coffee shops, restaurants and boutique hotels – including a pop-up espresso bar in Selfridges' London store – and is a favourite among baristas, including several UK champions.

Its well-equipped and stylish HQ has excellent training facilities and is responsible for training four of the top 20 finalists in the 2014 UK Barista Championships. In fact, anyone can pop along and join one of its home brewing courses, and it also has a great online shop for brewing apparatus and coffee gifts. And if you just want to sit and enjoy a cup, call in to Origin's own coffee shop, The Brew House, in Porthleven.

№82. EXTRACT COFFEE ROASTERS

www.extractcoffee.co.uk   T: **0117 9554976**

f/Extract Coffee Roasters   🐦/@extractcoffee

AVAILABLE
ONLINE

Extract Coffee Roasters began as a family venture serving home-roasted coffee from a cart on Bristol's iconic College Green.

Five years on, following the restoration of a 1955 60kg Probat roaster, it's proud to be producing coffee for the ever-hungry South West caffeine scene. A new roastery in the last 18 months has helped make Extract Coffee a destination for coffee enthusiasts, whether they're looking to buy a few grams of freshly roasted beans or taking part in a full training day of brew courses and tastings. As well as producing good coffee, it's also working to close the gap between farmer and consumer.

Day to day, the Extract roastery is aloud with the clinking of cupping bowls, humming of grinders, hissing of steamed milk and the slurps of noisy cuppers. Each new coffee that passes through the roasters is profiled, cupped, re-roasted, brewed and tasted by the whole roastery team in every possible way to find the optimum sweet-spot. Only then does it form part of its coffee offering.

Getting to know its product has taken Extract out to origin – to the farms of Brazil and Colombia to source new crops; to the final of the UK Cup Tasting Championship – where head roaster David Faulkner took home the title; and to the countless foodie festivals, cuppings and comps up and down the country.

Extract Coffee is on an ongoing crusade to find new ways of bringing exceptional speciality coffee to market. *'Since the beginning, getting fantastic coffee out the door was just the start,'* says David. *'Roasting is at the heart of everything we are as a business but barista training and servicing has developed into another integral part of what we do. We want our coffees, and the farmers who produce them, to be reflected in the best possible light. Perfectly crafted roasting is not always enough, which is why we developed "In Tamp We Trust" our barista training program, which is vital to our coffees-in-the-cup success.'*

In the ♥ of
good coffee

WORLD'S MOST
RELIABLE AND
ACCURATE DOSER
GRINDER

№83. YALLAH COFFEE

www.yallahcoffee.co.uk   T: 0773 8658079

f/Yallah Coffee Roasters   🐦/@yallahcoffee

AVAILABLE
ONLINE

You'll need your explorer's hat on to find Rich Blake and his vintage roaster, Beatrice. The oldest and prettiest roaster in Cornwall, Beatrice sits in an old barn on a friend's farm, hidden away at the end of a leafy lane in the Cornish countryside.

Of course you could catch Rich at one of the markets he attends in Truro or Falmouth. *'I like to talk directly to the customers about what I do,'* he says. The interaction, not just with seasoned coffee drinkers but anyone up for something new, genuinely pleases him and it's why his aim is to *'make coffee accessible for everyone, anytime and anywhere'.*

About three years ago, Rich was a production roaster at Extract in Bristol and before that he'd worked in the media and spent time living in France. But he'd always loved good coffee, and it was the opportunity to start working in a warehouse packing the stuff that really got him going in the industry. *'People were really friendly and helpful and I suppose I just wanted to keep on learning about it,'* he says. Rich soon moved on from packing to roasting and in particular, doing test roasting. *'I'd be working on hundreds of small batches, roasting and testing over and over again. It taught me a huge amount about coffee.'*

On the lookout for his own roaster, Rich found Beatrice decorating a shop window in Falmouth. *'She's a 1950s Swadlo and hadn't been used for 20 years. It took me six months to restore her.'* It also cemented his decision to move back to Cornwall, where his heart is.

He set up Yallah in May this year with a very clear mission to use only the best, single origin (strictly no blending) high altitude beans that have been sustainably sourced. His own adventurous spirit is reflected in his love of telling people about the journey of the bean and the people and the lands where it grew. He supplies smaller cafes and coffee shops, and if you can't catch him in Cornwall, he's also selling beans by post through his website. Coffees are grouped into Trust and Explore categories – Trust being very high quality, multi-appeal coffee and Explore for those who want to push the boat out and try something a bit more unusual.

And the name "Yallah"? It means "Let's Go!" in Arabic and is inspired by Rich's magical experiences of sipping coffee in Moroccan cafes.

№84. CRANKHOUSE COFFEE

AVAILABLE
ONLINE

O therwise known as the Cycling Barista, Dave Stanton is a familiar figure on the streets of Exeter, often found flying around from one coffee shop to another. But all that may change, now that the seasoned barista has set up his own roastery.

Originally from London, Dave and his wife spent more than a decade in Brisbane, Australia, where it was a love of cycling that put him on the coffee trail. *'The whole cycling/coffee phenomenon went berserk over there. You'd get cycling clubs with more than a hundred people and at the end of the ride they'd all go off to coffee shops,'* he says. *'That's what really sparked my interest in speciality coffee, and there are similarities between the cycling and coffee communities – I think it's the perfectionist thing.'*

In Brisbane, Dave discovered that some of the speciality coffee shops were front ends to roasteries – so he'd go in to buy a coffee

and find himself talking directly to the roaster as they worked. *'It's what I wanted to do,'* he says. But first there was some groundwork required. He returned to the UK three years ago and started working as a barista – spending all of his free time studying the art of coffee and working on roasting at home.

You could say that with an engineering background and a PhD in industrial robotics, Dave was well placed to get into the mechanics of roasting. *'I love the process, and understanding why things happen,'* he admits. Crankhouse Coffee was born after Dave acquired his first commercial roaster earlier this year. His intention is to be adventurous in his roasting and *'push the boundaries'*.

'There's some unbelievable coffee out there. Every now and then you get delivered a coffee that makes you go wow! It doesn't happen often, but there's huge potential, and I'm certainly aiming for that wow response.'

AVAILABLE ONLINE

www.wogancoffee.co.uk   T: **0117 9553564**

f/Wogan Coffee - Bristol   🐦/@wogancoffee

Wogan Coffee enjoys the privileged position of being the longest established and largest independent roaster in the South West. It's been sourcing, importing and roasting green beans in the heart of Bristol since 1970, when it was set up by Brian Wogan. And it's still very much a family affair, with Adrian Wogan at the helm and a third generation now involved in the business. The passion for nursing coffee through the roasting process is shared by a close knit team. Adrian says, *'We are proud to have some of the most respected palates, trainers and espresso machine technicians in the business and draw on our wealth of knowledge to deliver the best. We've recently welcomed five enthusiastic coffee lovers to the team and our head barista continues to receive many accolades.'*

At the heart of the operation is a classic 1968, 90kg Probat coffee roaster and in a supporting role (and for small batch roasts) is a recently added hand-built 30kg roaster.

Wogan Coffee is passionate about its beans and likes to have full control over the whole process, from sourcing to roasting to training. It works with farms from more than 40 origins around the world and every single one of its beans is carefully roasted by hand, by its master roaster, at the Bristol warehouse.

Wogan is constantly cupping new crops and one of its latest is from La Bastilla in Nicaragua – it's a single estate and Direct Trade coffee. A close involvement with producers has led to educational and sponsorship work and the team recently went to Nicaragua to present degree certificates to a group of its sponsored students.

₌86. CLIFTON COFFEE ROASTERS

www.cliftoncoffee.co.uk   T: 08452 606706

f/Clifton Coffee Roasters   🐦/@cliftoncoffee

AVAILABLE
ONLINE

Getting right down to basics, Andy Tucker has a carefully considered, and very precise, aim with his roasting: *'It's about treating the green coffee with the utmost attention to detail to ensure that we show its characteristics in the best possible way for the method in which it's to be brewed.'*

The company was formed in 2001 and you'll often find Andy roasting away at the heart of Clifton's warehouse on the outskirts of Bristol. Brick walls, concrete floors, utilitarian shelving and hessian sacks of exotically labelled beans create atmosphere, and in the middle of it all is Andy with his Diedrich roaster. A lot of sample roasting and tasting goes on at Clifton. *'We're looking for sweetness, body, acidity and something unique that makes that coffee stand out from the rest,'* he says. *'When sourcing our single origin coffees, we want them to speak for themselves.*

'Often we work on two different profiles for each coffee to allow customers to brew that coffee via an espresso machine or through various filter methods. There's more than one way to roast a coffee and the brew method dictates a lot of what a roaster needs to do. It's about the combination of airflow, heat transfer and time in the roasting drum in order to make that coffee work in the hands of the barista on their chosen equipment.'

Andy and the team at Clifton are also good at building relationships - both with baristas and the importers who bring the green beans into the country. They're also big on providing help and advice – including training – and work with top manufacturers like La Marzocco, La Spaziale, Mahlkonig, Mazzer, Fetco and Hario to provide the necessary equipment and service.

For over a decade Clifton has been at the forefront of the region's coffee industry, but there's a welcome modesty there too, as clearly the beans are the star. As Andy says, *'We don't want to add our personality to the roasting process, we merely want to ensure we select great coffee in the first place and find a roast profile that shows the flavour in the best possible way. We look for coffees that are great examples of their variety, process method, terroir, region and country. If anything, our style is perhaps best shown in the type of coffee we choose to buy, not in how we roast it.'*

AVAILABLE ONLINE

www.djmiles.co.uk   T: 0800 387948

f/Miles Tea & Coffee   🐦/@milesteacoffee

D J Miles is very experienced when it comes to importing and creating beverages as the company started life as a tea merchant back in 1888.

The team has been based in Porlock since the 1960s and it's not unusual to walk through the Exmoor village and catch the beautiful aroma of freshly roasted coffee from its roastery, which is housed in a converted stable block. If you visit the premises, you can peek in and see the two working roasters in action through one the windows. Roasting takes place every day, and the company supplies a range of clientele from top hotels, restaurants and businesses to private consumers across the South West.

The company has a dedication to quality that goes hand in hand with generations of experience, and it's a family run affair – the current chairman Derek Miles is the third generation of the Miles family. There's a traditional artisan approach to DJ Miles' work and, unusually, its tasters still use an old brass penny as the weight to measure out the coffee (and a silver sixpence as the weight for tea).

A mixture of bean suppliers is used; some sourced directly from the farmers, many through trusted brokers with relationships that stretch over 40 years. The beans come from around the world, with the majority originating in Central and South America and the Far East. Sustainability is important and DJ Miles aims to ensure that the coffee farmers receive a fair price for their beans.

The focus here isn't on the latest coffee trends, but on traditional values and providing high-quality blends that customers want to drink again and again.

88. RAVE COFFEE

www.ravecoffee.co.uk   T: **01285 651884**

f/Rave Coffee   🐦/@ravecoffee

AVAILABLE
ONLINE

Rave Coffee began in 2009 when Vikki and Rob Hodge decided to emigrate to Australia – leaving the corporate world to work with some of the best baristas and coffee roasters in Sydney, Australia. After two years drinking in as much knowledge and experience as they could, they returned to the UK to start roasting coffee, Aussie style.

The pair's Cirencester roastery was launched in January 2011 and has blossomed into a vibrant company with ten equally coffee-keen employees, all drawn to Rave by its passion and enthusiasm for great coffee.

With the arrival of the new Loring roaster and the already well bedded in Toper – both of which run under the watchful eye of Rob and his colleague Brooke Purdon from 8am to 7pm everyday – it'll be all hands on deck in the packing department as the team toils tirelessly to keep the coffee heading out of the door as fresh as is humanly possible.

Rave's fundamental aim when it comes to sourcing green coffee is to focus on variety, processing and unique flavours, using farms that produce small batch and micro-lots. Sustainable buying is also key, and the company is serious about ensuring a fair price is paid to farmers to encourage future business and develop strong relationships.

As well as roasting single origin and coffee bean blends and supporting individual cafes, coffee chains and five star airports, the guys also sell coffee wholesale across the globe. But whether supplying a few bags or a few tonnes, quality is always the focus.

SEASONAL SPECIALITY COFFEE. SOURCED DIRECTLY.

We source our coffee directly from growers to ensure an exceptional product which is ethical and sustainable. We roast in Cornwall on a Loring Smart Roast, the world's first environmentally friendly roaster. Our coffee is roasted lightly to enhance the individual characteristics that the growers have worked tirelessly to perfect.

Experience Origin at leading independent coffee shops & boutique hotels. Or buy via our website.

origincoffee.co.uk

ORiGiN®
coffee roasters

MEET OUR COMMITTEE

The South West Independent Coffee Guide's committee is made up of a small band of coffee experts and enthusiasts who, when they couldn't find a guide to speciality coffee venues in the region, decided to get together and create one ...

ANDY TUCKER

Head of coffee for Clifton Coffee Roasters, Andy is a SCAA qualified lead instructor and has spent over 12 years in hospitality and catering. *'I've focused on speciality coffee while working across Canada, Australasia, France and the UK - in a variety of retail and wholesale roles.'* he says, *'At Clifton I oversee the green coffee procurement and roasting facilities as well as managing our wholesale and education programme.'*

MAXWELL COLONNA-DASHWOOD

'An epiphany moment with coffee several years ago was just the beginning of my fascination with, and passion for, coffee,' says two-time UK Barista Champion and two-time world finalist, Maxwell. *'I love so much about coffee and the elements of its world, but it's coffee's potential as a culinary product that excites me most.'* Maxwell's coffee shop Colonna & Small's is in Bath and he also runs Dashwood Coffee Consultancy.

ED GOODING

Ed is the UK and Ireland sales manager for Bunn, which supplies top-notch coffee equipment across the globe. Ed says, *'I love a hobby, and while some of mine have come and gone (surfing and DJing for example) coffee remains a constant in my life. I'm fortunate to work in an industry that I love - and at a very exciting time. We are watching quality become the norm, which is fantastic. Oh, and I also enjoy wearing Lycra and drinking wine'.*

NICK COOPER

Nick's day job is as director at Salt Media, the South West boutique publishing company that hand crafts **food** magazine and *The Trencherman's Guide*. His obsession with coffee started 12 years ago when he was living and working in Sydney. A couple of barista courses and a lot of flat whites later he and his wife Jo returned to the UK to open an Aussie style coffee shop. They ended up creating Salt Media instead – but at least now he's got his own coffee guide.

A huge thank you also goes out to Tom Sobey at Origin Coffee for helping the committee and the Salt Media crew get the guide off the ground.